SHARKS

SHARKS

 Reader's Digest

The Reader's Digest Association, Inc.
Pleasantville, New York/Montreal

CONTENTS

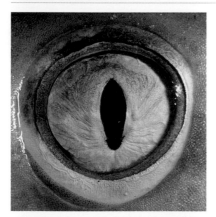

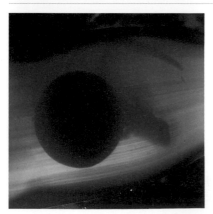

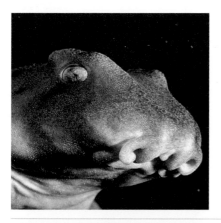

IDENTIFYING SHARKS 86

SHARKS AND PEOPLE 124

A Reader's Digest Book

Conceived and produced by Weldon Owen Pty Limited

A member of the Weldon Owen Group of Companies

The credits and acknowledgments that appear on page 160 are hereby made a part of this copyright page.

Printed in China

WELDON OWEN Pty Limited
PUBLISHER: Sheena Coupe
ASSOCIATE PUBLISHER: Lynn Humphries
PROJECT EDITORS: Libby Frederico, Greg Hassall
EDITORIAL ASSISTANTS: Vesna Radojcic, Shona Ritchie
ART DIRECTOR: Sue Rawkins
DESIGNER: Kylie Mulquin
PICTURE RESEARCHER: Annette Crueger
ILLUSTRATORS: Chris Forsey, Ray Grinaway, Gino Hasler, Frank Knight
INDEXER: Garry Cousins
PRODUCTION MANAGER: Caroline Webber
PRODUCTION ASSISTANT: Kylie Lawson
AUTHORS: Dr. Leonard Compagno (Chapters 1, 2, and 3); Dr. Colin Simpfendorfer (Chapter 4); Dr. John E. McCosker (Chapter 5); Dr. Kim Holland, Chris Lowe, Brad Wetherbee, Aaron Bush, and Carl Meyer (Chapter 6)

Library of Congress Cataloging in Publication Data

Sharks
        p.   cm. — (Reader's digest explores)
    Includes index.
    ISBN 0-7621-0041-9
    1. Sharks.   I. Reader's Digest Association.   II. Series.
QL638.9.S458   1998
597.3—dc21   97-46928

UNDERSTANDING SHARKS

SHARKS BELONG TO THE CLASS
CHONDRICHTHYES, ALONG WITH RAYS AND
THEIR MORE DISTANT RELATIVES, THE
CHIMAERAS. THEY HAVE EXISTED IN ONE
FORM OR ANOTHER FOR MORE THAN
450 MILLION YEARS. A LONG EVOLUTIONARY
HISTORY HAS FINE-TUNED THEIR DESIGN,
SUPERBLY ADAPTING THEM TO THEIR
MARINE ENVIRONMENT.

SHARK MYTHS AND FACTS

We all know what sharks are, don't we? Or do we? Most people in the modern world may not have much, if any, physical contact with sharks, but many have negative impressions of them that have more to do with myths, legends, and media images than with the actual creatures termed "sharks."

VICTIMS OF "BAD PRESS"

In the past three decades a great deal of new information has been uncovered about the lives of sharks, and our understanding of their biology, diversity, significance, and conservation status has changed dramatically. Yet overshadowing this quiet revolution has been a noisy media emphasis on the more sensational aspects of shark biology, particularly shark attacks. While this is a perpetuation of centuries of "bad press" regarding sharks, it is an unfair and inaccurate emphasis.

There are nearly 500 species of shark and they are extremely diverse in shape and biology. More than 80 percent of these are harmless and smaller than humans, not conforming to the stereotype image of the "man-eater" at all. In fact, the "average" shark is between 3 to 4¼ feet (90 to 130 cm) long at maturity; feeds on small fishes, crustaceans, and other invertebrates; and is very much a "man-avoider!"

Fortunately, the 1990s have seen an ongoing improvement in the perception of sharks among more enlightened sectors of the public. While the popular misconception of sharks as predatory killers has remained to some extent, more and more people are becoming aware that the shark attack problem is primarily a problem of humans attacking sharks. Worldwide, sharks attack fewer than 100 people a year, yet people kill over a hundred million sharks during the same period through uncontrolled commercial fishing.

WHERE SHARKS LIVE

Sharks live in most habitats in the sea and a few species also occur in fresh-water rivers and lakes. Most species occur in temperate and tropical waters on the shelves and slopes of continents and islands, from the shallows to depths of about 6,500 feet (2,000 m). A few

LEFT: The epaulette shark is a small, bottom-dwelling carpetshark that favors shallow, inshore water, particularly tide pools on coral reefs. It has short fleshy protuberances, known as barbels, on its snout near the nostrils, which may help the shark to find food.

species are oceanic and there are some that are found in high latitudes near polar ice. Most sharks occur in well-aerated waters with a relatively high oxygen content. Many sharks are fairly sedentary bottom-dwellers (benthic), while others swim restlessly inshore (littoral) and in the open ocean (pelagic).

HUMANS AND SHARKS

There is a growing awareness among biologists and conservationists of the enormous pressure many sharks face from human interference. Because of their long lifespan and relatively low fecundity, sharks are particularly susceptible to overfishing. Furthermore, as sharks are often the unintended bycatch of large fishing operations, a depletion in their numbers will not affect the viability of these operations and will tend to go unreported.

BELOW: The white shark, or great white shark, has come to symbolize all sharks in many people's minds, but it is not typical in terms of size or behavior. While the white shark is a formidable predator, its danger to people is exaggerated.

BELOW: Although it is the largest living shark, the whale shark is harmless to people. It feeds mostly on microscopic plankton, on or near the surface, and will allow divers to swim alongside it, as seen here in waters off the coast of Western Australia.

Escalating human encroachment into fragile coastal and riverine environments has also led to the pollution and destruction of important natural habitats for some species.

The study of sharks shares the same inherent problem as the study of any other large aquatic animals, namely that they are more difficult and expensive to study than equivalent terrestrial animals. Furthermore, shark research is poorly funded and supported, partly because of the sharks' enduring negative reputation but also because they are of relatively little economic importance to fisheries. Hopefully the growing worldwide interest in sharks among divers, conservationists, and biologists will promote a greater awareness of the problems they face and a wider acceptance of the need for global shark conservation.

WHAT IS A SHARK?

Sharks are highly evolved living representatives of a large and unique group of fishes—the cartilaginous fishes, or class Chondrichthyes (a term combining the Greek words for cartilage and fish). Cartilaginous fishes have a long evolutionary history, diverging nearly 500 million years ago from the bony fishes (class Osteichthyes), from which humanity has its ultimate origin.

LEFT: The typical external form of active sharks, seen here in the whitetip reef shark, has served sharks well over millions of years of evolutionary history. When it comes to surviving in a marine environment, sharks have few equals.

CHARACTERIZING SHARKS

Sharks are jawed fishes. Like all fishes they are aquatic, water-breathing vertebrates with a brain and spinal cord; fins; plate-like pairs of internal gills; and paired sense organs, including eyes, ears, and nasal organs. Unlike most bony fishes, sharks do not have swim bladders or lungs.

Sharks' jaws are simple but effective structures, consisting of paired upper jaws (palatoquadrates) and lower jaws (Meckel's cartilages). They are armed with transverse rows of hard teeth that are replaced slowly but continuously. These teeth are not in sockets, but attached to the jaws by soft tissue.

All sharks have paired fins—pectoral and pelvic—on the underside of the body. The pectoral, or breast, fins have a common structural origin to human arms and are located just behind the gill region of the head. The pelvic fins, the equivalent of human legs, are positioned on the rear of the abdomen just in front of the tail. In male sharks, each pelvic fin has a clasper, or copulatory organ,

for implanting sperm inside the vent (the common reproductive and excretory opening) of the female. The vent is located between the pelvic fins in both sexes. Most sharks have a cylindrical or slightly depressed head and body; a strong tail with a caudal, or tail, fin; one or two dorsal fins on their back; and an anal fin on the underside of the tail behind the vent.

The skeletons of cartilaginous fishes are composed of cartilage instead of bone, similar to the material found in the human nose and ears. In many species the cartilage is supported by calcified nodules (tesserae). Bone, or bone-like tissue, may be present in the scales and teeth of some shark-like fishes. The prominent bony scales, bones of the head, and bony fin rays of familiar bony fishes are absent in sharks. Instead their bodies are covered with small, tooth-like, placoid scales, often referred to as dermal denticles.

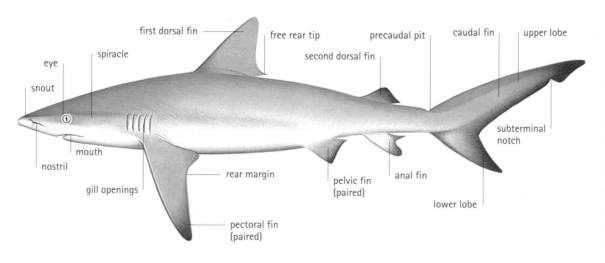

first dorsal fin — free rear tip — precaudal pit — caudal fin — upper lobe

spiracle — second dorsal fin

eye

snout

subterminal notch

mouth

nostril

gill openings — rear margin — pelvic fin (paired) — anal fin — lower lobe

pectoral fin (paired)

THE EXTERNAL FEATURES OF A SHARK

This Caribbean reef shark exhibits all the common external features of sharks. While there is great diversity in shape and size among the various species, most of these features appear in one form or another in all sharks.

SHARK CLASSIFICATION

Living shark-like fishes are in a taxonomic state of flux at present, and there are several alternative schemes for classifying them. Sharks are generally divided into eight major groups, often termed orders, based on common external features. These include the presence or absence of an anal fin, the number of external gill openings, the shape of the body and snout, the presence or absence of dorsal fin spines, and the position of the mouth. The eight orders are subdivided into smaller groups, or families, with variable numbers of species.

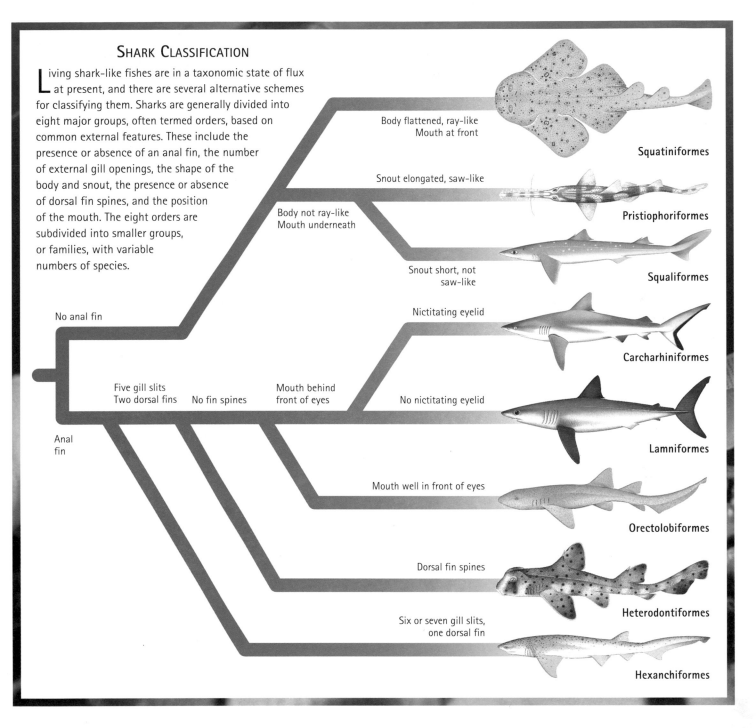

No anal fin

Body flattened, ray-like
Mouth at front
Squatiniformes

Body not ray-like
Mouth underneath

Snout elongated, saw-like
Pristiophoriformes

Snout short, not saw-like
Squaliformes

Nictitating eyelid
Carcharhiniformes

Five gill slits
Two dorsal fins

No fin spines

Mouth behind front of eyes

No nictitating eyelid
Lamniformes

Anal fin

Mouth well in front of eyes
Orectolobiformes

Dorsal fin spines
Heterodontiformes

Six or seven gill slits, one dorsal fin
Hexanchiformes

CLASSIFYING CARTILAGINOUS FISHES

Cartilaginous fishes are divided into two major groups: the elasmobranchs (sharks and rays) and the holocephalans (chimaeras). The term elasmobranch derives from the Greek words for plate and gills, an allusion to their plate-like gills which have five-to-seven pairs of separate openings on the sides of the head in sharks and on the underside of the head in rays. The term holocephalan derives from the Greek for whole and head, a reference to the way that chimaeras' upper jaws are fused to the braincase. The elasmobranchs and holocephalans have separate, parallel evolutionary histories that stemmed from a presumed, but unknown, common ancestor between 400 and 500 million years ago.

VARIATION AMONG SHARKS

When many people think of sharks, they tend to picture a large, aggressive white shark or mako, with fiercesome teeth and gaping jaws, cutting through the water like a torpedo. While there are number of restless, predatorial sharks that do conform to this stereotype, they are only part of the story. Sharks vary enormously in both shape and size, with more than 80 percent of sharks being smaller than human beings.

A MARVELOUS DIVERSITY

Sharks have an extraordinarily long evolutionary history during which they have fine-tuned their design to suit the varied habitats in which they live. Today's living sharks are a dazzlingly diverse lot and include tiny, deep-sea dwarves; flattened, ray-like bottom dwellers; graceful, streamlined, ocean swimmers; and huge, slow-cruising filter feeders with cavernous mouths.

Male sharks tend to be somewhat smaller than females of the same species, although a number of catsharks reverse this rule. Roughly 8 percent of sharks are dwarves, one of the smallest being the spined pygmy shark, which reaches 6 inches (15 cm) at maturity. The largest shark is the whale shark, reaching lengths of up to 45 feet (14 m). An "average" shark might have a mature size of about 30 inches (90 cm) long—hardly the monster of *Jaws* infamy.

White Shark
This highly active, torpedo-shaped mackerel shark is a powerful and efficient predator.

Bonnethead
This small hammerhead is an active coastal shark. It has a more rounded head than other species of hammerhead.

SHARK DIVERSITY

Sharks vary greatly in shape and size. This small selection of shark species, drawn to scale and compared with the size of a human diver, provides a glimpse of this marvelous diversity.

Tasselled Wobbegong
This small, flattened, bottom-dwelling carpetshark has fleshy tassels on its chin and jaw, which resemble weeds.

Bigeye Thresher
This streamlined, ocean-swimming mackerel shark is the second largest of the threshers. Like all threshers, it has a highly elongated caudal fin.

Pacific Sleeper Shark
This gigantic, slow-moving dogfish has a stout body and inhabits cold to temperate waters.

Silky Shark
This slender, oceanic requiem shark is a fast swimmer, capable of dramatic darting movements.

Longnose Catshark
This small, slender ground shark inhabits deep ocean and shelf waters.

Whale Shark
This massive, spindle-shaped carpetshark is the largest living fish. Despite its size it is harmless, filter feeding on plankton and small fishes.

Spined Pygmy Shark
This tiny, deep-water dogfish is one of the smallest living sharks.

EVOLUTION OF SHARKS

The origin of sharks and the other types of cartilaginous fishes is shrouded in mystery. As jawed fishes, their shape and structure link them to the bony fishes and their land-living relatives, the tetrapods (including amphibians, reptiles, birds, and mammals). However, the common ancestor of sharks and bony fishes is unknown. Furthermore, their relationship to other groups of extinct jawed fishes, including the placoderms (plate-skinned fishes) and the acanthodians (spiny-finned fishes) is not agreed upon by all contemporary researchers.

THE FOSSIL RECORD

One reason for uncertainty is that for most of their history sharks have left an incomplete and sometimes perplexing fossil record. A shark's cartilaginous skeleton is too soft to fossilize readily so whole fossil sharks are extremely rare. However, the hard parts, such as teeth and fin spines, fossilize easily and there is a rich fossil record of these. Fossils of sharks' teeth are particularly abundant as teeth are continually replaced throughout a shark's life. A single shark may shed tens of thousands of teeth in just a few years.

The first fossil shark teeth occur at the start of the Devonian, about 409 million years ago. By the end of this period, some 363 million years ago, sharks were relatively diverse and common in the fossil record. The first rare, whole-bodied shark fossils occur during the middle Devonian, about 380 million years ago.

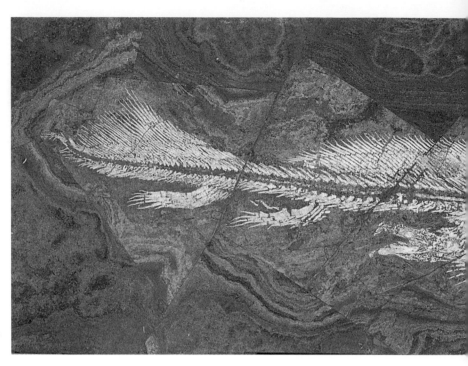

THE EARLIEST SHARKS

Cartilaginous fishes originated between 570 and 420 million years ago, near the beginning of the Paleozoic era. However, until the Devonian (the Age of Fishes) we have only scrappy fossil evidence in the form of scales and spines that suggests the presence of these ancestor fishes without revealing their form. One group possibly involved in the ancestry of sharks is the thelodont agnathans. These apparently jawless fishes had shark-like scales and, in some species, shark-like shapes.

ABOVE: A fossil of a Permian xenacanth Orthacanthus senckenbergianus, *found in a quarry in Germany. These sharks lived between 260 and 290 million years ago, and are believed to have been bottom-dwelling, fresh-water predators, capable of sudden dashes after prey.*

AN EARLY ANCESTOR

The long-extinct *Cladoselache*, which thrived during the Devonian, shares many physical characteristics with modern sharks. It is thought to have been a swift and powerful predator, capable of hunting large, fast-swimming fishes.

the derivation of rays from sharks. This stage ended with another catastrophic series of extinctions at the close of the Cretaceous, about 65 million years ago. The dinosaurs and many other vertebrates disappeared entirely, while sharks, rays, and chimaeras were considerably diminished in diversity.

The third stage occurred during the Cenozoic, from 65 million years ago to the present. This saw the evolution of all modern sharks, rays, and chimaeras, with a reshuffling of dominance within the shark groups and a revival of shark and ray diversity. An intriguing shark that evolved during this period was the megatooth shark *Carcharodon megalodon*. This relative of the white shark may have become extinct as recently as 13,000 years ago. It possibly grew as long as 30 to 45 feet (10 to 15 m), which would make it the largest macropredatory shark ever to have roamed the earth's oceans.

BELOW: This fossilized whorl of teeth belonged to the ancient shark-like Helicoprion, *which lived more than 245 million years ago. It is believed that new teeth formed in the rear of the mouth and rotated forward to form this unique whorl shape.*

EVOLUTIONARY TRANSITIONS

The evolution of cartilaginous fishes can be divided into three stages of expansion, or adaptive radiation, that were punctuated by major extinctions. The first, Paleozoic, stage began with an increase in the diversity of cartilaginous fishes in the Devonian and culminated in the Carboniferous, between 360 and 290 million years ago. By this time, cartilaginous fishes had differentiated into the holocephalans (chimaeras) and elasmobranchs, and were the dominant fishes in marine waters. The elasmobranchs included archaic, but already specialized, early sharks, and the first of the "true sharks," including hybodonts, xenacanths, and even a few modern sharks (neoselachians).

This golden age of cartilaginous fishes ended as the Paleozoic closed about 240 million years ago with a massive worldwide extinction of species. Very few sharks and chimaeras survived, but some of those that did became the precursors of all living sharks, rays, and chimaeras.

The second, Mesozoic, stage took place between 180 and 65 million years ago. This saw the extinction of the archaic sharks, a modest re-radiation of chimaeras, the great adaptive radiation of the modern sharks, and

ABOVE: This fossil tooth of the extinct shark Carcharodon megalodon *is almost 6 inches (15 cm) long. This is more than twice the size of a white shark tooth, leading to claims that the shark would have been almost 100 feet (30 m) long. This view, however, has since been discredited.*

RELATIVES OF SHARKS—RAYS

The members of the most numerous and diverse group of sharks are usually not considered to be sharks at all, at least in the popular view and even by many scientists. However, the 700 or so living species of ray, or batoids, are essentially flattened shark derivatives—"flat sharks" or "winged sharks." Rays are a diverse group. Some, at less than 4 inches (10 cm) long at maturity, are among the smallest cartilaginous fishes, while the manta, with a maximum "wingspan" of more than 18 feet (6 m), is one of the largest.

WHAT IS A RAY?

Rays are analogous to birds, which evolved from small terrestrial dinosaurs and developed enlarged, highly specialized wings from their pectoral appendages, which enabled flight. Similarly, rays are sharks that expanded their pectoral fins for underwater "flight," and in the process supplemented, or replaced entirely, their tails and caudal fins.

Rays are similar to sharks in basic body plan, but have modifications related to their specialized form and their largely bottom-dwelling life. Their pectoral fins are enlarged and fused onto the sides of the head over the gill openings, which are on the underside of the head rather than on its sides. These pectoral fins are flexible, mobile, propulsive organs with finely segmented supports (radial cartilages) and expanded muscles, capable of flapping up and down like wings. While the jaws of sharks are attached to the tongue skeleton (hyoid arch), in rays the lower tongue skeleton is separated from the upper. This allows a ray to accurately thrust its jaws forward to grab prey that appears under its head.

The shoulder and hip girdles of rays are wider than those of most sharks, and unlike sharks the shoulder girdle is fastened to the vertebral column to provide a firmer base for the expanded pectorals. In most rays the section of vertebral column between the skull and the pectoral girdle is partly or completely fused into a tube, which provides further support for the pectoral fins. In rays, the upper eyelids are fused to the eyeball, while in sharks they remain free.

EVOLUTION OF RAYS

The common structural features of living and fossil rays strongly suggest that all rays have a common ancestor. Rays evolved during the Mesozoic era, first appearing in the early Jurassic, some 200 million years ago. Fossil

LEFT: This electric ray is superbly camouflaged as it lies against a rock in Pacific waters off Mexico. These rays have large, paired electric organs in their pectoral disks, capable of producing powerful shocks.

BELOW: A diver with three stingrays off the Cayman Islands. If provoked, stingrays will defend themselves with the venomous, barbed spines on their tails. However, they are gentle, inquisitive creatures and will tolerate respectful divers.

evidence shows that the primitive Jurassic guitarfishes resembled today's living guitarfishes in external form as well as habitat, occupying the soft bottom of shallow continental seas. Of the living sharks, sawsharks may be the closest to a common ancestry with rays. While angelsharks appear ray-like, they are divergent in form and only distantly related.

HABITAT AND FEEDING

Rays are primarily bottom dwellers and many bury themselves beneath sand or mud. However, some of the more advanced species, such as mantas and eagle rays, are powerful swimmers capable of bird-like "flight" through the water and even, on occasion, the air.

Rays are generally found in habitats that support sharks and are more diverse than sharks at high latitudes (in the form of skates) and in fresh water. On the other hand, there are even fewer species of oceanic ray than there are oceanic sharks. The two largest ray

ABOVE: Common throughout the tropics, the majestic manta ray is one of the largest of all the rays. This filter feeder swims almost continuously with a powerful, graceful motion.

groups—skates and stingrays—complement each other in distribution. Skates dominate the deep slopes and inshore waters at high latitudes, while stingrays dominate fresh water and the tropics.

Rays feed mostly on small bottom organisms and their teeth never develop into the large, scissor-like cutters that sharks possess. However, there are some interesting variations of feeding behavior among rays. Some of the larger skates have strong jaws and moderate-sized, pointed holding teeth that allow them to eat large fishes and octopuses, while some electric rays use their electric organs to stun large fishes and swallow them whole. Eagle and cownose rays have large, plate-like crushing teeth and can crack hard-shelled mollusks such as clams and oysters. Sawfishes use their saw-like snouts to stir the bottom to reveal their prey. They have also been known to use these snouts to hit small fishes. The manta rays are plankton feeders, using gill filter plates and horn-like rostral fins on the front of their heads to strain small animals from the water.

CLASSIFICATION OF RAYS

All the rays can be placed in a single order, or superorder, known as Rajiformes or Batoidea. Within this group, living rays are variously ranked but conventionally divided into five major subgroups. Four of these—the sawfishes, electric rays, skates, and stingrays—apparently represent natural evolutionary assemblages with common ancestors. The guitarfishes, however, represent an artificial assemblage of relatively primitive rays, disputed by taxonomists but considered together here for convenience.

The sawfishes (Pristiformes, one family) are large rays with stout, shark-like bodies; small pectoral fins; stout tails and caudal fins; a pair of large, shark-like dorsal fins; and elongated, flattened, saw-like snouts with several pairs of large, pointed saw-teeth on either side. They are worldwide in distribution, occurring in warm, shallow continental seas and tropical rivers and lakes.

The guitarfishes (Rhinobatiformes, three or more families) are small to huge rays with fairly stout, shark-like bodies; small to large pectoral fins; stout tails and caudal fins; a pair of moderate-sized dorsal fins; and angular to bluntly rounded snouts. They occur worldwide in shallow to moderately deep, warm-temperate to tropical seas.

The electric rays (Torpediniformes, four families), or torpedoes, are dwarf to moderately large rays with flattened bodies, stout tails, and blunt snouts. They have large pectoral fins with paired, kidney-shaped electric organs, and most have one or two moderate-sized dorsal fins. They occur worldwide in shallow to deep, cold-temperate to tropical seas, primarily in continental waters.

The skates (Rajiformes, one to three families) are dwarf to moderately large rays with flattened bodies, large pectoral fins, slender tails, small caudal fins, and pointed

or blunt snouts. Some have one or two small dorsal fins near the end of the tail. They are found worldwide in shallow to extremely deep seas off continents and islands.

The stingrays (Myliobatiformes, at least eight families) are small to gigantic rays with flattened bodies, large pectoral fins, and slender to whip-like tails, usually with a stinging spine. Their snouts are angular to blunt, or divided into two branches. Some stingrays have a small dorsal fin near the base of the tail, and the caudal fins, if present, are small. Stingrays occur worldwide in shallow to deep, temperate to tropical seas, with a few oceanic species.

ABOVE: The bat ray is a stingray that frequents kelp forests and other inshore environments off temperate coasts. Its most distinctive feature is its long, whip-like tail, which has a stinging spine near the base. From below, the ray's external gill openings are clearly visible on the underside of its head.

BELOW: The fiddler ray is a guitarfish common to shallow waters off the southern coast of Australia. It is a bottom dweller, favoring seagrass meadows, but is also frequently seen near wharves and jetties. The fiddler ray survives well in captivity and is often kept in public aquariums.

ABOVE: The great skate, common to shallow coastal waters off the southern coast of Australia, is well camouflaged against the shallow sandy sea floor. It is the largest Australian skate and has a formidable array of thorny spines on its tail.

BELOW: A school of devilrays, closely related to the manta rays, seen from the air over Ningaloo Reef in Western Australia. This aerial view clearly reveals these rays' unusual snouts, which are divided into two branches.

RELATIVES OF SHARKS—CHIMAERAS

Termed silver sharks in Japan and ghost sharks in Australia, chimaeras are relatively obscure cartilaginous fishes. Little is known about them biologically with the exception of the elephantfishes, which support relatively large fisheries in the Southern Hemisphere. The split between elasmobranchs (sharks and rays) and holocephalans (chimaeras) occurred early in the evolution of cartilaginous fishes, some 400 million years ago, and today's chimaeras are the remnants of a mighty host of fossil holocephalans that challenged the sharks for dominance during the Carboniferous.

COMPARING SHARKS AND CHIMAERAS

Chimaeras are not particularly shark-like in appearance, having a compressed, tadpole-like form similar to some deep-water bottom-dwelling fishes. Shallow-water chimaeras are more silvery than sharks, but deep-water chimaeras tend to have the somber, dark hues of deep-water sharks and rays. Unlike sharks, chimaeras have an erectile first dorsal spine and fin, and three pairs of tooth plates that continually grow and wear down. These tooth plates protrude from the mouth much like rats' teeth and probably inspired the names "ratfish" and "rabbitfish" for some species.

Chimaeras have a soft external gill cover with a single, rear gill opening on each side, while sharks have five to seven pairs of separate external gill openings. Male chimaeras, like male sharks, have claspers on the pelvic fins, but they have an additional lobed clasping organ in a pocket in front of each pelvic fin, and a bizarre knocker-shaped clasping organ on the forehead. These are used to grip the female during copulation.

ABOVE: This ratfish is a species of shortnose chimaera that occurs in shallow to deepish water in the northeastern Pacific Ocean. Its intricate color pattern may serve as camouflage when it visits rocky inshore areas. Most shortnose chimaeras are found in deep water and are uniformly colored.

RIGHT: *Longnose chimaeras are uncommon fishes found exclusively in deep water. As a result there are no known photographs of live specimens. What little information we have about these elusive fishes has come from specimens inadvertently caught during deep-sea trawl fishing.*

CHARACTERISTICS OF CHIMAERAS

Living chimaeras are bottom dwellers that grow to a length of about 2 or 3 feet (60 or 90 cm). They are never found in fresh water, nor are they active coastal or oceanic swimmers. Most of the fifty or so recognized species live in deep water on the slopes of continents and islands. As such, they are rarely observed and our knowledge of them is patchy at best.

The few species that have been observed alive swim forward relatively slowly by flapping their large, leaf-shaped pectoral fins. They use their other fins for steering and maneuvering. Chimaeras feed on small bottom organisms, including invertebrates and small fishes, and may be preyed upon by larger sharks. All chimaeras are oviparous, laying their eggs in elongated, spindle-shaped cases with side flaps.

IDENTIFYING CHIMAERAS

Although they represent less than 5 percent of all cartilaginous fish species, chimaeras are reasonably diverse. The fifty or so recognized species comprise one order (Chimaeriformes) and three well-defined families: elephantfish (family Callorhinchidae), longnose chimaeras (family Rhinochimaeridae), and shortnose chimaeras (family Chimaeridae).

Elephantfish have silvery bodies; elongated, plow-shaped snouts; shark-like caudal fins; and short second dorsal fins. They are found in temperate inshore and offshore waters of the southern continents.

Longnose chimaeras, often evocatively referred to as spookfish, have whitish to dark brown or black bodies; long, pointed snouts; long second dorsal fins; and caudal fins that taper to a narrow point. These strange-looking fishes are found only in deep water, occurring worldwide in cold-temperate to tropical seas.

Shortnose chimaeras, also known as ratfish or rabbitfish, have silvery, spotted, dark brown or black bodies; short, blunt snouts; long second dorsal fins; and narrowing caudal fins. They occur inshore in temperate waters at higher latitudes but are more common in temperate and tropical seas below 650 feet (200 m), on shelves, deep slopes, and sea mounts.

RIGHT: *The elephantfish, also known as the plownose chimaera, is so named for its unmistakable, plow-shaped snout. The size of the snout suggests that the sensory organs contained within it are highly sensitive and may be used for finding prey and possibly also for social interactions. There are only three species of elephantfish worldwide, all confined to temperate waters.*

THE SHARKS' WORLD

SHARKS CAN BE FOUND IN ALL THE
EARTH'S OCEANS FROM THE WARM
WATERS OF THE TROPICS TO THE FRIGID
SEAS OF THE POLAR ZONES, RANGING
FROM SHALLOW COASTAL WATERS
TO THE DARK DEPTHS OF THE OCEAN
FLOOR. SOME SPECIES ALSO SPEND
SHORT PERIODS OF TIME IN
FRESH-WATER RIVERS AND ESTUARIES.

SHARKS IN THEIR ENVIRONMENT

Sharks are primarily marine fishes, inhabiting a world from which humans are largely excluded. While we readily travel the surfaces of the oceans, our penetration into the watery world of sharks is imperfect and incomplete. Submarines and submersibles conveniently preserve our terrestrial environment under water, but the contact they allow with sharks is very limited. Swimming and diving with sharks allow us much greater contact, but ultimately reinforce just how different their world is to ours. We simply do not have the variety of sensory equipment to perceive the underwater world as sharks do, and consequently it appears a profoundly alien place.

AN EVER-CHANGING ENVIRONMENT

The complexity of water masses in the world's oceans provides a rich and varied sensory environment for sharks. There are constant variations in temperature, concentration of dissolved organic and inorganic chemicals (including oxygen and salt), and ambient sound, light, and movement. Changes in bottom and coastal topography and fluctuations in the earth's magnetic field provide navigational obstacles and cues. At the same time, sharks must share this world with an abundance of other animals and plants, interacting with an endless procession of potential predators and prey.

SUPERBLY ADAPTED

Sharks are superbly suited to the constantly changing environment that cradles and nurtures them. Most species, with the exception of some bottom dwellers, are about equal in density to water and expend very little effort to keep from sinking. The denseness of water provides resistance against which sharks can work their tails and fins to move, and induces drag to slow their movements. Water also provides dissolved oxygen for shark respiration, and dissolves and dissipates the byproducts of their metabolism.

The sharks' basic design was established before they even evolved, as the first crude fishes became more mobile and began to develop evolutionary answers for active life in

RIGHT: A snorkeler swimming with a whale shark. Humans are beings of sight and sound, and our other senses are more poorly developed. When we clumsily penetrate the seas we are half-blind and deaf, awkwardly coping with artificial breathing and loss of heat. When we encounter sharks in this world, we can only marvel at their sleek and easy movements.

LEFT: The effortless suspension of this sandbar shark in waters off Hawaii is a tribute to hundreds of millions of years of shark evolution. Its streamlined design and light, flexible cartilaginous skeleton allow it to move through its surging marine environment with breathtaking ease.

the water. Sharks added a deceptively simple, yet versatile, skeletal system, devoid of heavy, clumsy external armor or intricate bones. Some of the Devonian sharks already showed the sleek, spindle-shaped elegance of the modern makos, at a time when fishes were often tank-like in their armor plating and, probably, their movements. Sharks never developed extensive armor, instead enhancing a wide range of sense organs inherited from their common ancestry with other jawed fishes. This enabled them to develop a sophisticated, multi-sensory approach to their environment. Shark brains increased in size and complexity along with these sense organs.

A shark's streamlining and protective coating of small, plate-like scales combat drag, while the fins and bodies provide propulsion, maneuvering, and lift. Sharks evolved a system of tooth production and replacement that proved enormously versatile, and adapted sharks to a wide variety of feeding strategies. They also developed a range of relatively complex behaviors, including social patterns, synchronized movement, and means of chemical and visual communication.

In addition, sharks developed a high-value reproductive strategy that produces relatively small numbers of self-reliant offspring. Young sharks are born fully formed, without the need for postnatal care or for defense against potential predators by parents. As a result, parental energy can be concentrated in the prenatal nurture of unborn young or the production of large eggs.

That the sharks' design is a success is written in the rocks, and this fossil record illustrates the resilience of sharks in the face of vast catastrophes. They not only survived, but ultimately flourished at times when other fish groups became inconsequential relicts or disappeared from the earth entirely.

EFFECTS OF DEPTH AND PRESSURE
Some sharks are able to tolerate a wide range of depths, flourishing in both inshore and deep-water environments. The white shark is primarily an inshore and oceanic species but it also penetrates deep water on the continental slopes. On the other hand, the

bluntnose sixgill shark is a bottom-dwelling, deep-water species, but it is also found inshore in cold temperate waters and even near the surface in the tropics.

The majority of deep-water shark species, however, are confined to deep water, and have adapted specifically to this cold, inky black environment. Deep-water sharks are often blackish or chocolate-brown in color, and some have luminous light organs. These organs may be useful for protection, for attracting prey, or for making themselves more conspicuous during social interactions.

The eyes of deep-water sharks are usually large and flash green or yellow. They are not adapted for form vision but are probably extremely sensitive to low levels of light. The dorsal and caudal fins and tails are often small and weak in deep-water sharks, while abdomens are large with huge, oily livers.

Many deep-water sharks are relatively inactive and are geared to a long life, reproducing very slowly in a stable, low-energy environment. Adaptations to high pressure are not obvious, and sharks do not have the problems of deep-water bony fishes with swim bladders, which pop when depressurized. Abrupt increases in temperature and light level may be more difficult to cope with, as these sharks are physiologically adapted to low temperatures and only the intermittent light produced by other organisms.

ABOVE: The shortfin mako is a restless ocean swimmer. With its spindle-shaped body and short pectoral fins, it is capable of bursts of speed of more than 22 miles per hour (35 km/h) and can leap up to 20 feet (6 m) into the air.

FRESH-WATER SHARKS

Very few species of shark penetrate fresh water beyond the influence of tides, and only two groups of large requiem shark occur in fresh-water rivers and lakes far from the seas. Of these, the bull shark is the most successful in fresh water, and is often found in warm-temperate to tropical lakes and rivers. Rivers sharks are far less common, with only a few species in Asia and Australia, but some of these may by exclusive to fresh-water rivers.

A number of other shark species are considered marginal, occasionally penetrating brackish estuaries and the lower reaches of rivers with permanent sea access. Few, however, will venture far into rivers. In general, sharks are not biologically suited to the highly variable conditions found in fresh-water environments and are unable to compete ecologically with the many animals that thrive there.

SYMBIOTIC RELATIONSHIPS

Sharks and their parasites form swimming communities, and in many cases the hosts and parasites are so well adjusted that little or no damage is evident. A number of bony fishes are found in close association with large, active pelagic sharks. These include pilot fish, remoras, the cobia, and various jacks. These fishes can feed on scraps from sharks' meals and take advantage of a shark's strong swimming ability. Some fishes may gain a boost by swimming in a shark's wake, while remoras can hitch a ride by using sucking disks on their heads. In return, some remoras eat parasites from the sharks' skin.

HABITATS AND DISTRIBUTION

We know very little about the relationship between sharks and the varied habitats in which they live. What we do know, however, is that sharks occupy a wide range of habitats in the sea, but are limited in distribution in certain respects.

LIMITS OF DISTRIBUTION

Sharks are most varied in temperate and tropical seas, in the shelf waters of continents and islands and on the adjacent deep-water slopes. There are fewer species in the sunlit upper reaches of the open ocean, very few in the deep ocean basins, and barely any at all in very deep water. Compared with the vast array of bony fishes, amphibians, reptiles, mammals, and birds that inhabit fresh water, sharks are represented in this environment by only a handful of species. And of these, only the bull shark is common and wide ranging, found in a variety of temperate and tropical fresh-water habitats, including rivers and lakes.

As modern sharks are relatively large fishes, they do not compete with bony fishes and invertebrates in habitats suitable for very small animals. Consequently there are no inshore shoals of small pelagic sharks, no tiny crevice or hole dwellers, no small sharks occupying tiny territories on coral or rocky reefs, no minute sharks with very small mouths that feed on small invertebrates, and no small sharks that hide in kelp or engage in symbiotic relationships with invertebrates.

Where sharks do thrive is in the role of moderate-sized to large marine predators. As such, they broadly overlap those habitats dominated by bony fishes and invertebrates, and feed extensively on the inhabitants of these micro-niches.

RANGE OF HABITATS

A wide variety of species occur in coastal marine waters. Bottom-dwelling and littoral sharks patrol off sandy open beaches, and may even enter the breakers. Smoothhounds target benthic invertebrates while larger species, such as spotted sevengill sharks, bronze whalers, sand tigers, dusky sharks, tiger sharks, and white sharks, prey on marine vertebrates.

In temperate seas, sharks occupy a variety of habitats along rocky coastlines, inshore rocky reefs, and kelp forests. Some species, such as catsharks, wobbegongs, and hornsharks, live on the bottom and may rest in caves and crevices, dispersing to feed on invertebrates. Active pelagic species, such as sevengill and white sharks, may prowl the reefs and kelp.

Shallow and deep bays, lagoons, estuaries, and other protected habitats are favored by many species of shark, large and small, as are river

BELOW: As large predators, sharks reign supreme in the world's marine environments. Here a group of blacktip sharks hunts small bony fishes in waters off the Bahamas.

RIGHT: The tasselled wobbegong spends most of its time on the bottom of inshore rocky reefs, feeding on fishes and invertebrate prey. This wobbegong is superbly camouflaged as it lies in wait on the bottom of the Great Barrier Reef in northeast Australia.

BELOW: Sand tiger sharks frequent the mainly shallow waters of bays and rocky reefs. They feed on small to large bony fishes and even, on occasion, other sharks.

Coral reefs in the tropics attract several well-known species of shark, including lemon and tiger sharks, great hammerheads, nurse and tawny sharks, coral catsharks, longtailed carpetsharks, and a variety of reef sharks. Even whale sharks may appear to feed when reefs bloom with plankton. Offshore coastal waters provide habitat for various small to large littoral and benthic sharks, out to the edge of the continental and insular shelves.

DEEP-WATER LIMITS

The soft bottoms of deep slopes, underwater ridges, and sea mounts support a range of deep-water sharks above a depth of about 6,550 feet (2,000 m). These include sleeper, lantern, gulper, frilled, goblin, sixgill, and sharpnose sevengill sharks, as well as catsharks and false catsharks. Relatively few species are found below these depths.

In the open ocean a few sharks inhabit the upper reaches, from the surface to 1,650 feet (500 m). These include large requiem sharks, such as blue, silky, and oceanic whitetip sharks, as well as threshers, makos, white sharks, salmon sharks, and various dwarf kitefin sharks, including the pygmy and cookiecutter.

mouths and deltas. Such habitats are rich in life, and many coastal sharks use them for breeding, feeding, and as nursery grounds. Some sharks enter and depart bays with the tides, and even large white sharks will swim in the intertidal zone of bays that empty at low tide.

Sharks are most diverse and abundant in tropical waters, particularly near the coast, and many species of shark will penetrate very close to the shore. This lemon shark is in water off the Bahamas barely deep enough to cover it.

Few sharks range into the depths of the ocean basins, with the possible exception of the pygmy and cookiecutter sharks. Sharks are very rare between a depth of 10,000 and 30,000 feet (3,000 and 9,000 m) and are not found at all in ocean trenches, although a gulper shark was photographed from a bathyscaphe on the ocean floor at a depth of more than 13,000 feet (4,000 m) and a Portuguese shark was recorded at a depth of about 12,140 feet (3,700 m).

FACTORS DETERMINING DISTRIBUTION

Present shark distribution is strongly influenced by the location of land masses; the temperature, oxygen level, and salinity of water masses; and the presence of other organisms, including prey. Only sleeper sharks are known to survive under the Arctic ice cap, while few species can tolerate low oxygen levels, fresh water, or unusually high levels of salinity.

Worldwide environmental changes during the past 8 million years (including continental drift and changes in sea level, water temperature, bottom composition, rainfall patterns, and the distribution of prey species) have had a huge influence on the distribution of sharks. Some species that were once worldwide in distribution are now restricted in their range. The snaggletooth shark is now found only in the Indo-West Pacific and the sand tiger shark has disappeared from the eastern Pacific Ocean.

ABOVE: *The bottom-dwelling nurse shark favors the inshore waters around tropical reefs. Largely inactive during the day, it feeds on invertebrates and fishes once night falls.*

response to changing temperatures. The white shark is unique in the extent of its distribution, ranging from the inshore tropics to the Arctic and sub-Antarctic seas, and from intertidal zones to continental slopes and the open ocean. This enormous range may be related to its size, high level of activity, ecological position as a top predator, and partial warm-bloodedness, all of which allow it to roam widely and tolerate a vast range of temperatures.

SHARK NUMBERS

We know very little about the worldwide abundance of sharks, although we can say with confidence that some species are, or were, enormously abundant. The blue shark, spotted spiny dogfish, and possibly the shortfin mako, oceanic whitetip, silky, and soupfin sharks, have, or have had, world populations comprising millions of individuals. However, anything more than a rough estimate of numbers for these sharks is impossible, as the only figures we have to go by are statistics from fisheries that are incomplete and difficult to interpret.

Another problem in gauging abundance is the inaccessibility of many species. Some tropical inshore and fresh-water sharks are known only from a handful of records in the last 150 years, and some deep-water and oceanic sharks may be even more elusive.

In the face of increasing worldwide pressure from fisheries, estimates of abundance are crucial in conserving and managing shark numbers. At present, however, we only have vague estimates for a handful of species and much work remains to be done.

ABOVE: While the greatest diversity of shark species occurs near the shore, some sharks, such as the oceanic whitetip, prefer the open ocean. This sluggish shark is an opportunistic feeder, eating whatever it can catch.

RIGHT: The inaccessibility of deep-water habitats makes it difficult to estimate the abundance of shark species, such as the kitefin shark, that live there.

Water temperature is an important factor in the diversity and distribution of sharks in coastal waters and in the upper reaches of the oceans. There is a striking decrease in shark diversity moving from the tropics to the poles.

In some species, changes to coastal water temperatures bring about local and long-range migrations as sharks actively seek out waters within a suitable temperature range. Warm-water coastal and oceanic sharks often range into higher latitudes in summer and retreat towards the equator in winter, while cool-temperate species may demonstrate the reverse pattern. Similarly, other coastal species may move between inshore and offshore waters in

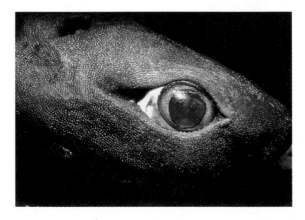

ACTIVITY PATTERNS OF SHARKS

The activity patterns of most sharks are poorly known. However, from short term observations and clues provided by their shape, it is clear that activity levels vary enormously between species.

BENTHIC AND PELAGIC SHARKS

For convenience a broad distinction is often made between sedentary, bottom-dwelling sharks associated with the sea floor (benthic) and highly active sharks that swim restlessly off the bottom (pelagic). This is certainly a useful distinction and one that holds true for a number of species. Some sharks, such as the mako and great white, are highly active and seldom rest from the moment they are born, while at the other extreme there are species such as angelsharks and wobbegongs that are exclusive to the bottom, and spend part of their lives lurking in ambush on the sea floor.

Many species, however, are not so neatly categorized. Some benthic species, such as hornsharks, use their muscular pectoral and pelvic fins to clamber over the bottom and can swim sluggishly from place to place. Other species, such as the swellsharks, rest on the bottom during the day, but are more or less

LEFT: The Gulf catshark is found in southern Australian waters, on or near the seabed. Largely inactive during the day, these sharks swim short distances during the night in search of prey.

BELOW: Oceanic whitetip sharks are more or less exclusive to the open ocean. They cruise slowly from the surface to depths of about 500 feet (150 m), often accompanied by pilot fish.

ABOVE: The scalloped hammerhead is a versatile, wide-ranging shark, found in most tropical and temperate seas. It moves freely between shallow coastal waters and the open ocean, from close to the surface to depths of up to 1,000 feet (300 m). Many large pelagic sharks cover vast areas in the course of their normal activities.

active swimmers at night. Some benthic species, such as the bluntnose sixgill shark, are found offshore in deep water on the continental and insular slopes, and at times they apparently hover well above the bottom. To some extent a benthic shark's level of activity is determined by its size. Some small species, such as certain wobbegongs, frequent the same limited range all their lives, while larger species, such as the nurse shark, may swim over a large area.

Pelagic sharks are often divided into coastal (littoral) and oceanic species and there are a number of species that are exclusive to one or other of these environments. Several species of reef shark are exclusively littoral, found within approximately 650 feet (200 m) of the coast in waters bounded by the continental shelves, while other species, such as the mako and oceanic whitetip shark, are exclusively oceanic.

However, not all pelagic sharks are as easily categorized as this, with many species, including the white and whale sharks, occupying both coastal and oceanic waters. Also, while some oceanic sharks occur in the sunlit upper layer, others, such as the cookiecutter, descend well below it, even reaching the abyssal plains at depths of more than 6,500 feet (2,000 m). Although pelagic sharks are often characterized as restless, or free swimming, this is not always the case. While most pelagic species do indeed swim almost continuously, others, such as the megamouth shark, can hover in midwater and some may even rest on the bottom.

LATITUDINAL DISTRIBUTION

Sharks are sometimes classified as tropical, temperate, or polar species, and there is certainly a clear correlation between shark diversity and distance from the equator. Diversity is greatest in the tropics and steadily decreases as one moves toward the poles.

Divisions along latitudinal lines, however, do not take full account of variations in water temperature caused by water depth and seasonal changes. For example, the temperature of tropical water at a depth of 1,000 feet (300 m) is roughly equivalent to that of surface polar water. As a result, cold-adapted sharks that occupy surface water in high latitudes may also inhabit cold, deep water in temperate and even tropical regions, much as there are cold-adapted flora on the slopes of tall tropical mountains.

Seasonal migrations also blur the distinction between tropical, temperate, and polar sharks. Tropical inshore and oceanic sharks often ride warm currents, such as the Gulf Stream in the North Atlantic, well north or south of the tropics. Likewise, cold current systems such as the Benguela Current off the west coast of southern Africa allow temperate inshore species to range into the tropics. Sharks may also migrate in response to longer term climatic events such as the El Niño phenomenon.

TROPICAL SHARKS

Sharks abound in marine waters of the coastal tropics, particularly in the Indo-West Pacific, which has the most species of shark anywhere in the world. Tropical coastal waters of the Atlantic and Eastern Pacific have fewer species of shark, but this is partly due to a general decrease in diversity in these regions over the last 60 million years. Moving away from the coast, sharks species are less diverse, although there are more epipelagic species in the tropics than in colder waters.

As previously noted, many tropical sharks range well beyond the tropical latitudes. A number of predominantly tropical species ride warm currents well north and south of the tropics and may seasonally invade temperate waters as warm-water masses shift poleward.

THE TROPICAL MARINE ENVIRONMENT
Tropical coastal seas teem with life, as do tropical forests on land. The warm, sunlit waters of the inshore tropics change little between seasons. High, near-constant water temperatures provide externally warmed aquatic animals with optimal conditions for growth, reproduction, diversity, and high levels of activity. Under such conditions the pace of

evolution is rapid, and there tend to be a larger number of tropical aquatic species inhabiting a wider variety of habitats and ecological niches than occur in cold surface waters.

Tropical diversity extends to large, predatory marine animals, including the sharks. Marine inshore habitats in the tropics may have dozens of species of shark with specialized ecological roles and widely different body forms, while comparable inshore habitats in colder seas may have only a few ecologically equivalent species.

ABOVE: Active tropical sharks, such as this silky shark, inhabit surface waters of the open ocean and may follow warm currents from the tropics to temperate regions.

BELOW: The whale shark is often found near the surface in tropical waters, where it filter feeds on plankton.

BELOW: *Coastal tropical waters provide optimal conditions for the growth, development, and reproduction of marine animals, and sharks are most numerous and diverse in this environment. This Caribbean reef shark is a typical requiem shark, the dominant family in tropical waters.*

Tropical coastal sharks show no obvious adaptations for warm tropical waters, and it is likely that warm-temperate and tropical coastal waters were optimal for the adaptive radiation of most shark groups. The colder waters of the higher latitudes and ocean depths appear to inhibit the diversification of sharks, as do very warm tropical waters. The warmer the water, the lower its oxygen content, and as sharks require highly oxygenated water in order to breathe, they tend to avoid water that is warmer than 90°F (32°C).

TROPICAL SPECIES

Although the open oceans generally contain fewer species of shark than coastal waters, a relatively large number of sharks inhabit open waters in the tropics. The gigantic whale shark and the somewhat smaller megamouth shark both occur regularly in tropical oceanic waters, but are also found in coastal waters off the shelves of continents and islands. These large, filter-feeding sharks also range into temperate waters by following warm currents.

Tropical oceanic waters are also home to several species of large, predatory mackerel and ground sharks, including the mako, thresher, oceanic whitetip, blue, and silky sharks. These active, free ranging sharks inhabit the sunlit upper reaches of the open ocean. At greater depths, tropical oceans also support a number of small dogfish sharks. The spined pygmy and cookiecutter sharks, as well as several species of sleeper and lanternshark, all inhabit cold, deep oceanic water in tropical regions.

It is in tropical waters close to the shore that sharks are at their most diverse. A great variety of littoral sharks inhabit such areas, including the spotted sand tiger shark and many houndsharks, weasel sharks, hammerheads, and requiem sharks. The last of these is the dominant group of sharks in the coastal tropics and includes such common species as the silky, silvertip, bull, and blacktip sharks, the bronze whaler, and several species of reef shark. Some of these tropical littoral sharks favor coral reefs, while others frequent muddy estuaries, bays, river mouths, and sandy beaches.

Benthic sharks are also diverse in the tropics and include slender, cylindrical, reef-dwelling species, such as the longtailed and collared carpetsharks, as well as inshore catsharks, such as the wide-ranging coral catshark. There are also flattened bottom dwellers, such as the wobbegongs and a few angelsharks, although the latter are mostly a temperate-water group. Tropical waters support several more generalized benthic-adapted species, such as hornsharks, nurse and zebra sharks, and the Australian blind sharks. Frilled sharks also occur in the tropics, but are restricted to deep, cold waters near the bottom of the continental and insular shelves.

SHARKS IN COOLER WATERS

While there is a marked decrease in the diversity of sharks the farther one moves from the tropics, it is not always possible to precisely characterize sharks by their latitudinal range. Water temperature is a more important factor in the distribution of sharks than latitude alone. Cool to cold water occurs at the surface in north and south temperate zones and in the Arctic and Antarctic oceans, but also at depth in temperate and even tropical seas.

Structural adaptations of sharks to cold waters are not obvious, but may include the partial warm-bloodedness of some mackerel sharks, which allows a high level of activity (see pages 50–51). Those cold-dwelling, deep-water sharks that are externally warmed share a number of physical characteristics that reflect their low metabolism and consequent low levels of activity. Such characteristics include enlarged livers and abdomens, relatively weak muscles, small fins and tails, and reduced calcification.

SHARKS IN TEMPERATE WATERS

A number of large, active sharks range widely from the tropics to temperate waters and beyond. Littoral and pelagic species, including the requiem sharks, the hammerheads, makos, threshers, whale sharks, and spotted sand tiger sharks, all inhabit tropical waters but extend into warm-temperate seas along current systems, sometimes as far as the Arctic Circle. These movements, however, are dictated by the flow of warm currents, and such sharks avoid cold waters.

Coastal temperate waters tend to be cool to cold with marked seasonal variations. Compared to tropical waters, these are harsh environments with greatly reduced ecological diversity, and consequently fewer species of shark are found there. There are, however, some littoral species that are apparently well adapted to such cool coastal areas, including the basking and spotted sevengill sharks, some houndsharks, some species of dogfish shark, and some benthic catsharks, Australian carpetsharks, and angelsharks.

A number of species that are considered temperate range well beyond the latitudinal limits of these zones. The partially warm-blooded porbeagle and salmon sharks apparently prefer cool temperate water but can tolerate very cold water and range into the Arctic and possibly the Antarctic circles. The white shark, an opportunistic and partially warm-blooded top predator, has perhaps the widest distribution of any shark. While it breeds in warm-temperate seas, it ranges far into the tropics as well as high latitudes. When sharks range widely, they tend to position themselves in the water column according to the temperature of the water. The blue shark, for example, swims near the surface in temperate seas but moves into increasingly deep water as it extends into the tropics.

SHARKS IN POLAR WATERS

The distribution of sharks in the cold waters of the Arctic and Antarctic circles is poorly understood. Few sharks occur in these waters, and those that do are primarily temperate sharks, such as the porbeagle, salmon, and basking sharks. Only two species—the Greenland and Pacific sleeper sharks—are known from under the Arctic icecap and around the shallow, inshore Arctic waters. Sleeper sharks are also found off sub-Antarctic islands but have not been observed inside the Antarctic Circle. These sharks are wide ranging and also occur in deep water in cool- to warm-temperate, and possibly even tropical, seas.

ABOVE: *The huge, filter-feeding basking shark is a highly migratory nomad, apparently well adapted to cold waters. Basking sharks sporadically inhabit cold coastal areas to exploit the rich blooms of plankton that appear there from time to time.*

RIGHT: *The great white shark is possibly the widest-ranging living shark. While considered a temperate species, it is able to cope with cold water at high latitudes and warm water in the tropics.*

INSET: *The bluntnose sixgill shark may rival the great white in terms of wide distribution. This large shark is generally found near the bottom in cold-temperate seas, but also occurs on seamounts and insular slopes in the tropics.*

DEEP-WATER SHARKS

While knowledge of the distribution of deep-water sharks is poor, it is apparent that a number of species occur exclusively in the cold, deep waters of the continental and insular slopes. Some deep-water species, such as the sixgill shark, are wide ranging in temperate and tropical zones and may even reach Arctic waters. Others, however, are limited to cool-temperate, or tropical and warm-temperate regions.

The deep-water environment is cold and dark, but for some shark groups it may represent their optimal environment as they are more diverse in such waters than anywhere else. These include a number dogfish sharks, as well as some catsharks, frilled sharks, and sixgill and sevengill sharks. Pygmy sharks, tiny deep-water dogfish, make nightly migrations from depths of almost 5,000 feet (1,550 m) to the surface as they follow their food supply.

How Sharks Work

From swift and powerful oceanic swimmers to sluggish bottom-dwellers, sharks are biologically diverse and sophisticated. Their streamlined external features and flexible skeletons combine with an efficient respiratory system and dazzling array of sensory organs to ensure mastery of their watery world.

SHARKS IN MOTION

Many common and familiar sharks are graceful swimmers and some barely stop moving from the moment they are born. Sharks inherited a common body form and way of moving from primitive jawed fishes, but these have been modified over time to suit a wide range of habitats and activity patterns.

SIZE AND SHAPE

Compared to bony fishes, sharks are relatively large creatures, although fewer than 20 percent of living species are larger than human beings. The ancestral body form of living sharks, similar to that of primitive bony fishes, is the littoral type, meaning adapted to an active, coastal life. This is characterized by a moderately elongate, cylindrical, or slightly flattened head; cylindrical trunk; and stout, long tail. It can be seen in the sand tiger shark, leopard shark, and many requiem sharks, all active swimmers in coastal environments, but all capable of resting on the bottom when necessary.

Benthic (bottom-dwelling) sharks exhibit a number of body modifications. In the extreme cases of angelsharks, wobbegongs, and rays, the head and trunk are greatly flattened and expanded laterally. Some bottom-dwelling sharks, including blind, nurse, and hornsharks, are only moderately flattened and may use

LEFT: The body of the Pacific angelshark is modified for a bottom-dwelling existence. It is highly flattened with expanded, ray-like pectoral fins. The two dorsal fins are unusually small and situated far back near the tail.

LEFT: The gray reef shark, seen here swimming in coastal South Pacific waters, retains the basic body form inherited from primitive jawed fishes hundreds of millions of years ago. With its cylindrical body, long tail, and slightly flattened head, it is well suited to an active, coastal life.

their specially adapted pectoral fins to clamber over the seabed. Others, including longtailed carpetsharks and several species of catshark, have relatively short cylindrical heads and trunks, and greatly elongated tails. Some of these sharks are crevice dwellers and clamber over the bottom of reefs, while others rest on soft sandy or muddy seabeds.

Deep-water sharks of the slopes, including sleeper, bramble, and gulper sharks, tend to have a cylindrical or slightly flattened head, a greatly elongated body that is cylindrical or somewhat compressed, and a short, weak tail. These sharks also have an enormous liver charged with squalene oil, which serves as a float. Some oceanic deep-water sharks, such as the cookiecutter and crocodile shark, also have a long abdomen and liver float, but they are generally more spindle shaped and have smaller fins, stronger tails, and more symmetrical caudal fins. The frilled shark is more radically modified for this environment, having a long, compressed, eel-like body between its short, rounded pectoral fins. These fins may be used to lunge after prey such as squid.

Finally there are the pelagic sharks. Some of the more active epipelagic (upper ocean) species, such as the oceanic whitetip and pelagic thresher shark, have cylindrical bodies similar to those of coastal sharks, except that the pectoral fins, and often the first dorsal fin, are more elongated and broad tipped. This adapts them to an active but slow-cruising life, interrupted by brief dashes after food or to escape from predators.

Highly active pelagic species, such as the mako and white shark, have very streamlined, spindle-shaped bodies with conical heads, stout trunks, and flattened tails with strong side keels. They cruise slowly but efficiently and are capable of sudden bursts of high speed when necessary. Filter-feeding basking sharks have similar bodies but are much larger, being modified for relatively slow cruising at the surface while straining plankton through their open mouths. Another filter feeder, the whale shark, is a converted bottom dweller and has a flat head, spindle-shaped body, and flattened tail. It is slow cruising but highly active, attending plankton blooms and concentrations of small fishes.

RIGHT: Few marine creatures can rival the mako for sheer hydrodynamic efficiency. With its stout, spindle-shaped body; short, stiff pectoral fins; and powerful, symmetrical tail, it is superbly adapted for a nomadic existence spent roaming the oceans.

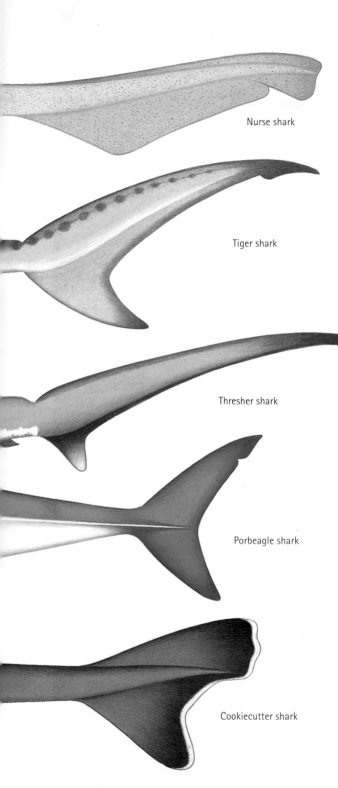

SHARK TAILS—VARIATIONS ON A THEME
Closest to ancestral form are the tails of tiger and nurse sharks, with their long upper lobes—a design the thresher shark has taken to extremes. The porbeagle's short, symmetrical tail is versatile, suited to slow cruising punctuated by sudden bursts of speed. The cookiecutter's tail is typical of an active deep-water shark.

THE FINS AND TAIL

All sharks have two sets of paired fins—the pectoral and pelvic fins. Sharks also have two to four unpaired fins—the caudal fin, one or two dorsal fins, and, in most species, an anal fin. Sharks' fins vary enormously in size and shape between species, but all serve to propel the shark through the water and to adjust its movements along all three axes.

The tail, with its lobed caudal fin, is the primary propulsive organ in sharks, its sideways movement providing forward thrust. Tails and caudal fins vary greatly in shape and provide clues to a shark's pattern of activity.

In all living sharks, the vertebral column extends into the caudal fin. In the case of benthic sharks and those that float in deep water, the vertebral column is nearly straight (or directed downward in angelsharks) and the lower caudal lobe is low. In active sharks, the vertebral column is elevated into the caudal fin, which is high and more or less crescent shaped (much like those of swift-swimming tunas or swordfish). The upper lobe of the caudal fin in thresher sharks is greatly elongated and sickle shaped and is used as a whip for stunning prey as well as for swimming. The zebra shark also has a greatly elongated tail, which is low and strap-like, but why it is elongated isn't known.

HOW SHARKS SWIM

The variety of movements of which a shark is capable with its full complement of fins is complex and not well studied. What is apparent is that the coordinated actions of the fins and body are fluid, precise, and extremely well integrated. Sharks swim by curving their entire bodies from side to side in a gentle arc, alternating direction as they move. More slender, elongate sharks, such as the blue shark, may undulate their body in an S-shaped curve, while stout, spindle-shaped sharks, such as the great white shark or shortfin mako, exhibit less pronounced side-to-side movements.

The large muscles of the trunk and tail are arranged in W-shaped bands around the vertebral column, and these contract alternately on either side to produce movement. Both the head and tail move from side to side as the

ABOVE: Blue sharks swimming in waters off California demonstrate the graceful, S-shaped movements typical of such slender sharks.

RIGHT: From behind, the view of a whale shark is dominated by its powerful caudal fin. That the whale shark has developed a tail this size is not surprising given the massive bulk that must be propelled through the water. The whale shark is a slow swimmer and spends most of its time at the surface, where it filters plankton and small fishes from the water.

body curves, and the sides of the tail and caudal fin push against the water, providing thrust along the longitudinal axis of the body.

The rate and extent of these movements can be increased or decreased to vary the shark's speed. By flexing their fins to increase drag, sharks are able to brake suddenly, allowing them to stop and hover. Sharks maneuver by twisting their bodies and by flexing their fins, and some can suddenly bend their bodies in a U-shape, enabling them to change direction completely within the length of their body.

Sharks' fins have streamlined cross-sections somewhat like aircraft wings, thick and rounded in front and tapering to a fine edge at the rear. In many sharks, the pectoral and pelvic fins are additionally convex on top and concave below, providing lift as the shark moves forward. Shark fins generally have a rear notch and a free rear tip that can be moved sideways (in the case of dorsal and anal fins) or up and down (in the case of pectoral and pelvic fins). The fins themselves are flexible and have internal muscles that allow them to bend and tilt while the shark is maneuvering or braking.

TEETH AND JAWS

A shark's teeth and jaws are more than just weapons. They are versatile manipulatory organs and, in the absence of tentacles, arms, or fingers, they are a shark's primary means of interacting with the environment. While teeth and jaws are a shark's chief feeding organs, they may also be used in social interactions (including courtship and copulation), for defense against predators, and for investigating and manipulating the objects around them.

VARIETIES OF TEETH

As far as we know, sharks feed entirely on other animals, ranging from tiny plankton to whales far larger than themselves. This variety is reflected in the wide range of tooth shapes found in modern sharks.

A primitive type of tooth found in many fossil sharks has a single slender cusp, a number of smaller cusps either side of it, and a long, flat base. Similar teeth are still found in certain modern sharks (such as frilled sharks, catsharks, and deep-water sand tiger sharks) that consume small fishes and other animals. These sharks use their long, thin teeth to impale their prey before eating them whole.

Many species of shark attack prey too large to be eaten whole, tearing off chunks of flesh instead. The white and tiger sharks have huge, broad, serrated teeth superbly suited to this feeding strategy. Many dogfish sharks have small, overlapping, compressed, sharp-edged teeth in the lower and sometimes upper jaws. Together these function like a sawblade and can be used to cut chunks out of prey. Cookiecutter sharks have large, highly specialized, saw-like cutting teeth in their lower jaw. When these sharks bite, they suck onto the prey with their

ABOVE: The teeth of a sand tiger shark are long, narrow, and needle-like, ideal for impaling small prey prior to eating them. All sharks feed on other animals—plant material found in shark stomachs is likely to have been accidentally digested when feeding on animal prey.

RIGHT: The huge, serrated teeth of great white sharks are brutally efficient when it comes to tearing chunks of flesh from prey.

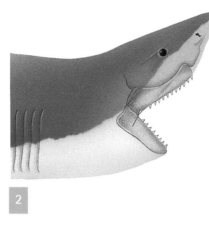

1

2

3

BITING ACTION OF THE WHITE SHARK

1 Prior to an attack, the upper jaw is firmly attached to the skull.

2 As the shark approaches its prey, the head is raised and the lower jaw is simultaneously dropped.

3 As the shark lunges, the entire jaw mechanism is detached and thrust forward.

lips and swivel around, removing a plug of flesh. In this way, these tiny sharks can attack large fishes and even whales. Other species, such as the dusky shark, combine broad cutting teeth in the upper jaw, with long, thin, gripping teeth in the lower jaw. Such an arrangement is ideal for catching large fishes, sharks, and rays.

Bottom-dwelling sharks that feed on hard-shelled invertebrates have specialized teeth for crushing shells. In the case of smoothhounds (such as the gummy shark) and hornsharks, the cusps on some or all of their teeth are greatly reduced or absent. These low, flattened teeth can be used as a mill to crush the shark's hard-shelled prey.

Filter feeders, such as the whale, basking, and megamouth shark, have small, hook-like teeth. These are not used for feeding but may have a function in social interactions.

REPLACING TEETH

Shark teeth are analogous to disposable razor blades—they have a short functional life and are replaced as they break or become worn. Shark teeth are arrayed in rows transverse to the jaws and the rim of the mouth. New teeth are continually formed in the gums inside the mouth and move outward. At the same time the oldest teeth reach the outer edge of the jaws and drop off as the connective tissue anchoring them to the gums is reabsorbed. The rate of replacement is unknown for most species, but experiments with captive lemon and hornsharks suggest that each tooth lasts from less than a month to about a year.

VARIETIES OF JAWS

Shark jaws are simple but effective, consisting of a pair of upper and lower jaw cartilages. The upper jaw is loosely suspended under the skull and is connected to the lower jaw at the outer rear corners. The upper jaw often overlaps the lower jaw in an overbite.

In general, modern sharks have mobile upper jaws, but the amount of mobility varies. Hornsharks and carpetsharks have grooves in the skull, along which the jaws slide forward. In other species, such as the great white shark, the jaws are more mobile. During an attack, the jaws move downward and are simultaneously thrust forward, producing an awesome bite.

Just as shark teeth vary greatly in shape, depending on the shark's diet and method of feeding, so too do their jaw cartilages. Sharks with small impaling teeth usually have relatively slender jaws and species with large cutting teeth or tooth bands tend to have deep, stout jaws.

HOW SHARKS BREATHE

Sharks breathe by extracting dissolved oxygen from water that passes through their gills. At the same time metabolic wastes (including carbon dioxide, carbonic acid, urea, and ammonia) are discharged into the water. Typically, water enters the mouth cavity (pharynx), flows through the internal gill openings into the gills, and is expelled through the external gill openings, or gill slits. As oxygen is far less concentrated in water than in air (approximately 1/30 the volume), a shark requires a huge amount of water to breathe, compared with the amount of air we land-based vertebrates require to fill our lungs with oxygen.

HOW GILLS WORK

The gills (or branchial region) consist of the skeletons of the gill and tongue arches; associated muscles that operate the gill pump; and the skin, blood vessels, and connective tissue which make up the gill septa and gill filaments. Gill filaments are thin, plate-like structures arranged in line with the flow of water through the gill cavities. They have a rich supply of blood vessels, which receive deoxygenated and waste-laden blood directly from the heart. This blood flows into lines of tiny capillaries in the gill filaments, which are arranged in such a way that the blood flows in the opposite direction to the inflowing water.

This forms a countercurrent exchange mechanism in which dissolved wastes in the blood diffuse into the water, while deoxygenated hemoglobin in the red blood cells picks up oxygen molecules from the water. The newly oxygenated blood then flows from the capillaries into blood vessels that supply the head, trunk, fins, and tail.

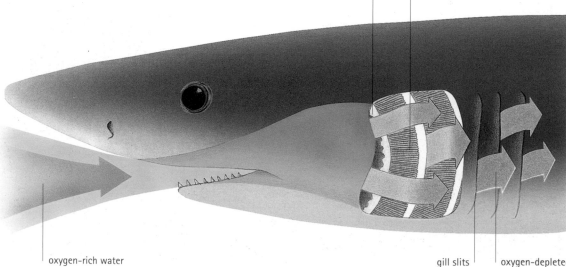

gill arch   gill filaments

oxygen-rich water

gill slits   oxygen-depleted water

GILLS IN ACTION

As water flows into a shark's mouth and through the internal gill openings, it ventilates the gill filaments, which are richly supplied with blood vessels. The flow of water and blood in opposite directions allows oxygen to be extracted from the water and metabolic waste to be extracted from the blood.

LEFT: When open to expel deoxygenated water, the large external gill openings of a whale shark clearly reveal the thin, plate-like gill filaments inside. Whale sharks have spongy filters at the gill arches, which filter small prey from the water.

MOVING WATER THROUGH THE GILLS

In order to absorb enough oxygen, sharks need to maintain a good flow of water over their gills. Some sharks generate much of this flow through constant forward movement—a process known as ram ventilation. As the shark moves forward, water enters the mouth, fills the pharynx, and ventilates the gill filaments. All sharks can benefit from ram ventilation while moving, but some highly active species, such as mackerel sharks and some requiem sharks, rely almost solely on this process to breathe during normal activities. Great white sharks, for example, barely stop moving from the time they are born. Although they can hover motionless for brief periods, they must soon start moving again in order to breathe.

THE GILL PUMP

While ram ventilation is an effective breathing strategy for sharks who are constantly on the move, most species are less active, spending at least some of the time resting on the bottom, sleeping, and hovering motionless. These sharks supplement the process of ram ventilation by way of an active, muscular gill pump, which generates a steady flow of water over the gills when the shark is not moving forward.

The gill pump works like a set of bellows, taking water into the pharynx and pumping it through the gills. Water enters the mouth as the muscles of the tongue and gill arches depress the floor of the mouth, increasing its capacity. Other muscles then close the mouth and contract the pharynx, causing water to exit through the internal gill openings, fill the gill cavities, and ventilate the gill filaments. A valve behind the teeth in the upper jaw stops water from flowing back out of the mouth while the pharynx is contracted. External muscles on the gills then contract to squeeze the water through the gill filaments and out the external gill openings, and the cycle is repeated.

Some bottom-dwelling sharks have enlarged spiracles with anti-backflow valves, which allow water to enter and to be pumped out of the pharynx while the mouth is closed. In this way, such sharks are able to process food or lie buried in ambush on the bottom without having to "hold their breath."

RIGHT: In order to force water through their gills, white sharks swim forward with their mouths open, a strategy known as ram ventilation. White sharks rely on this process to breathe and must remain more or less constantly on the move from the moment they are born. Restraining them may cause distress, or even death, from inadequate oxygen intake and the buildup of metabolic waste.

SKIN DEEP

A shark's skin serves many purposes. It contains the shark's innards; protects the shark from infection and damage; provides streamlining and anchors muscles; plays a role in camouflage and display; and produces dermal denticles, teeth, spines, sense organs, glands, and their secretions.

THICKNESS AND COMPOSITION

While a shark's skin is often a fraction of an inch thick and relatively tough, there is a tremendous variation among species. In some deep-water lanternsharks and gulper sharks the skin is thin and papery, while in the case of mature whale sharks, it can be more than an inch (2.6 cm) thick and extremely tough. Skin thickness may also vary within individual species. Female blue sharks have much thicker skin on their backs than males, and it has been suggested that this may help protect the female's delicate muscle tissue from bites during mating.

Shark skin is richly supplied with nerves, blood vessels, and sense organs. It consists of an outer layer (epidermis) with multiple layers of cells, and an inner layer (dermis) comprised of cells in a network of tissue fibers. Pigment cells (chromatophores) are present in the dermis, while glandular cells and multicellular glands occur in the epidermis.

Specialized glandular cells are present in sheaths of skin around the fin spines of dogfish sharks, and these produce toxins that can cause pain and even allergic shock when a person is struck by a spine. Deep-water sharks have luminous organs (photophores) in their skin. These modified glands contain light-producing cells and cells that function as lenses. Together these function much like miniature flashlights.

BELOW: A shark's scales are often referred to as denticles, which means a tooth-like projection. This close-up view of a nurse shark's skin clearly reveals the tooth-like nature of these scales. The dark patches reveal where old denticles have been shed.
INSET: The spines on each of a hornshark's dorsal fins are formed by secretions from the inner and outer skin layers.

RIGHT: *Sharks that dwell on the bottom of rocky reefs, such as this swellshark, are often colored so that they blend in with the rocks and marine plants around them. The skin coloration and patterning is produced by special pigment cells in the skin, known as chromatophores.*

PLATE-LIKE SCALES

Sharks have plate-like scales, known as dermal denticles, which are anchored in the skin and protrude from it. Denticles are protective and generally cover the entire external surface of the body, as well as all, or part, of the fins and mouth cavity. They have an external crown, a base anchored in the skin, and often a stalk-like support to elevate the crown above the skin. Denticles are periodically shed as new ones grow out through the skin.

In bottom-dwelling sharks, the denticles are often enlarged and very rough, but in many free-swimming, oceanic sharks they are small, with parallel ridges on their crowns. These small denticles serve to cut down drag by smoothing the flow of water over the shark. Teeth, fin spines, gill rakers in basking sharks, and clasper spines are all derived from denticles and are therefore technically part of the skin. They develop at the interface of the epidermis and dermis as mineralized and collagenous secretions from both skin layers.

BODY MARKINGS AND CAMOUFLAGE

The color and body markings of sharks derive from pigment cells in the dermis. Unlike the brilliantly colored bony fishes on tropical reefs, sharks tend to be somber colored. Their colors and color patterns are often cryptic, allowing them to blend in with their environment and concealing them from enemies and prey.

Pelagic sharks generally have uniform dark upper surfaces and white lower surfaces, which counterbalance the effects of light and shadow in the water and make these sharks relatively inconspicuous when viewed from below or above (see page 75). Deep-water sharks are often dark brown or black, while inshore bottom-dwelling sharks on rough seabeds often have mottled, spotted color patterns that blend in with rocks, reefs, or marine plants. Some sharks have black or white fin tips or dark spots above their pectoral fins that may serve to advertise their presence to other sharks, and which can be very conspicuous when combined with swimming displays.

CONTROLLING BODY TEMPERATURE

Water is a good conductor of heat, and aquatic animals tend to either lose or gain heat rapidly, depending on the temperature of the water around them. In most cases, sharks are warmed or cooled externally (ectothermic), and have a variable internal temperature that is approximately equal to the temperature of the water around them. Water temperatures range from slightly below freezing in high latitudes and in deep water, to more than 86° F (30° C) in the inshore tropics.

GENERATING HEAT

A shark's large trunk and tail muscles generate heat while it swims, and active sharks produce more heat than sluggish ones. However, because sharks lack insulating covering, the heat that is generated tends to rapidly dissipate to the surrounding water.

Marine mammals and birds have a constant body temperature well above that of the water. Their blood is warmed internally and they are insulated by their fur, fat, or feathers. The only sharks known to approximate warm-bloodedness are lamnid sharks (mackerel sharks of the family Lamnidae), such as the white shark and mako. While parts of their body have a consistently higher temperature than the surrounding water, they lack the insulation of mammals and their internal temperature is not constant.

These internally warmed (endothermic) sharks have modified circulatory systems that

ABOVE: *Unlike sharks, marine mammals such as sea lions have a thick, insulating layer of blubber or fur and are able to maintain a constantly warm body temperature.*

allow them to elevate the temperature of various organs (including the eyes, brain, stomach, and muscles of the trunk) for greater efficiency. In this way they are able to achieve a degree of warm-bloodedness while avoiding the high-energy costs of true warm-bloodedness.

The mechanism works through a process of heat exchange and requires energy generation by the muscles. The main heat exchanger is in the trunk muscles, where arteries supplying cold blood to the muscles run parallel to veins draining warm blood from the muscles. The cold incoming blood is warmed by the warm outgoing blood, resulting in a retention of heat within the muscle mass. While this system does not maintain a constant internal temperature, it does keep the temperature of selected organs above that of the water.

PATTERNS OF ACTIVITY

As most sharks are warmed or cooled externally, the simplest way for them to control their body temperature is to position themselves in water of a favorable temperature. Sharks at the surface can use warm surface water and sunlight for warmth and can cool themselves by diving down a short distance. Lamnid sharks may do likewise, but because they have some control over their internal temperature they are less reliant on this strategy. However, in order to generate the energy that fuels their complex heat exchange mechanism, they must remain more or less constantly on the move.

In general, sharks that operate at a low internal body temperature (such as deep-water sharks and those in polar seas) are sluggish and have a much lower metabolic rate than tropical sharks. Conversely, ectothermic sharks that live in the inshore tropics (including many requiem

and hammerhead sharks) can be highly active, and may elevate their body temperatures further with bursts of fast swimming. While such sharks are obviously not "cold-blooded," their body temperature is dictated by their surroundings. Some of these sharks can tolerate only warm water and migrate with the seasons accordingly. They may be stunned, or even killed, if they suddenly swim into a cold-water mass such as that produced by upwelling.

Similarly, cold-blooded sharks found inshore at high latitudes (such as sleeper sharks) are apparently intolerant of warm-temperate waters and occur at lower latitudes only in cold, deep water. Predictably, the degree of control that lamnid sharks have over their body temperature allows them to tolerate a wider range of temperature than most other sharks.

LEFT: As most sharks are at the mercy of the surrounding water temperature, one way they can warm themselves is to seek out warm surface water. This silky shark, a tropical requiem shark, is making the most of the sun over the Bahamas.

RIGHT: Some mackerel sharks, such as this great white, are able to maintain a body temperature higher than the water around them. This allows them to range more widely, and to be more active and efficient predators, than cold-blooded sharks.

THE ANATOMY OF A SHARK

The sleek exterior of a shark hides a variety of internal organs and cavities, fish-like in nature but with many features unique to sharks. A shark's body is supported by a cartilaginous skeleton, consisting of a braincase (enclosing the brain, inner ears, eyes, and nasal organs); a long vertebral column; paired cartilages that support the jaws, tongue, and gill arches; girdles that support the pectoral and pelvic fins; and the fin skeletons.

INSIDE A SHARK

A shark's body includes a cavity containing the heart (the pericardial cavity), which is just below the gills, and a trunk cavity (the visceral, or pleuroperitonal, cavity), which begins below the esophagus and contains other internal organs. The shark's head and trunk enclose a tubular gut, which includes the respiratory and digestive systems. It begins in the head at the mouth and ends at the vent, or excretory opening, between the pelvic fins.

A shark's mouth opens into the pharynx, which is connected to the esophagus and leads into the stomach. The stomach often extends rearward through part or all of the length of the visceral cavity and then doubles back on itself, connecting to the first part of the intestine (the duodenum) by way of a narrow, tubular section known as the pylorus. The duodenum is in turn attached to the valvular intestine. A shark's intestine is short, but its surface area and capacity to absorb vital elements is greatly increased by its spiral valve.

The valvular intestine extends rearward to the rectum, which discharges solid waste into a common reproductive and excretory chamber, known as the cloaca. The waste is ultimately expelled through the external opening of this chamber, known as the vent. Connected to the rectum is a tubular rectal gland, sometimes referred to as a third kidney, which excretes excess salt into the rectum.

The visceral cavity also contains a central gall bladder (which is connected to the stomach by a bile duct) and the liver, which is often very large and extends rearward to fill the lower part of the visceral cavity (see box). The spleen is located at the rear of the stomach

and the pancreas lies next to the pylorus. Paired kidneys are found in the upper wall of the visceral cavity and drain liquid waste into the ureter. The waste ultimately drains into the cloaca through a variety of ducts, different in males and females.

Below the kidneys are the reproductive organs—testes and their ducts (including the ductus deferens, seminal vesicle, and sperm sac) in males, ovaries and oviducts in females (see page 80). Male sharks also have a pair of external reproductive organs, known as claspers, which are used during copulation to deposit semen inside the female.

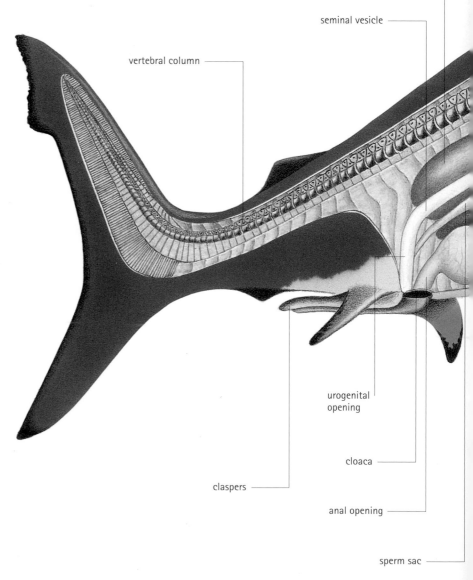

kidney

seminal vesicle

vertebral column

urogenital opening

claspers

cloaca

anal opening

sperm sac

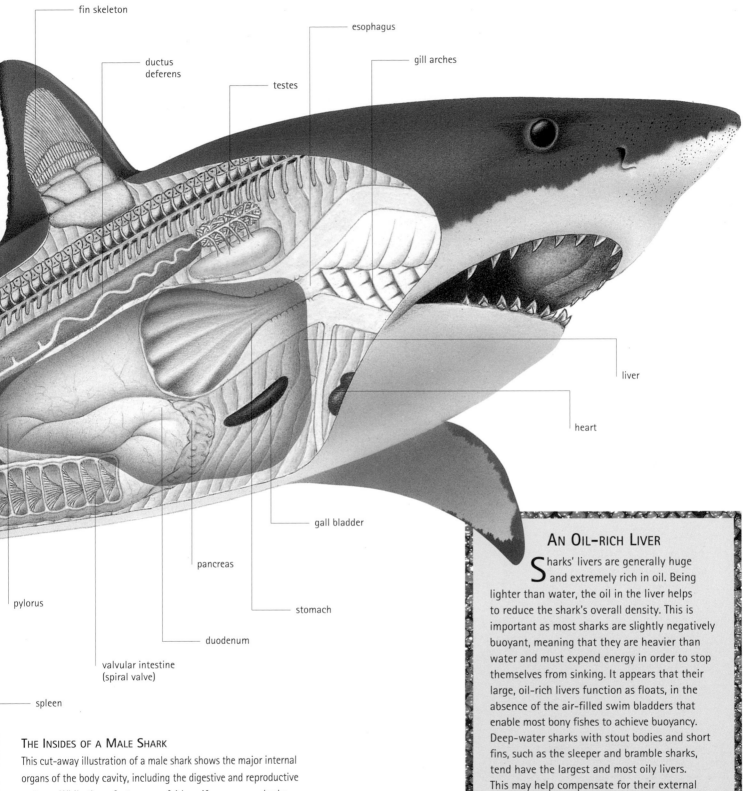

fin skeleton

ductus
deferens

esophagus

testes

gill arches

liver

heart

gall bladder

pancreas

pylorus

stomach

duodenum

valvular intestine
(spiral valve)

spleen

THE INSIDES OF A MALE SHARK

This cut-away illustration of a male shark shows the major internal
organs of the body cavity, including the digestive and reproductive
systems. While these features are fairly uniform among sharks,
there is some internal variation between species. This shark is
intended as a generic example only, showing basic anatomical
details, and is not supposed to represent any specific species.

AN OIL-RICH LIVER

Sharks' livers are generally huge
and extremely rich in oil. Being
lighter than water, the oil in the liver helps
to reduce the shark's overall density. This is
important as most sharks are slightly negatively
buoyant, meaning that they are heavier than
water and must expend energy in order to stop
themselves from sinking. It appears that their
large, oil-rich livers function as floats, in the
absence of the air-filled swim bladders that
enable most bony fishes to achieve buoyancy.
Deep-water sharks with stout bodies and short
fins, such as the sleeper and bramble sharks,
tend have the largest and most oily livers.
This may help compensate for their external
form, which provides them with less lift than
sharks with larger fins.

The Five Senses

The traditional five senses—touch, taste, smell, sight, and hearing—are apparently well developed in sharks and similar to those of other vertebrates. In addition, sharks have several other less familiar senses (see pages 58–61). Where sharks really excel is in the variety and complexity of their sense organs, and in the integration of sensory information within their nervous system to produce a rich and complex picture of their world. The incredible evolutionary success of sharks through time may be partly explained by this well-developed and integrated system of senses.

It must be emphasized that our understanding of shark senses is limited. Few live animals have been studied in detail, and what we do know is based only on sharks that are easily maintained in captivity, as well as a few free-ranging species (mostly requiem sharks) whose responses to sensory stimuli have been observed in the field.

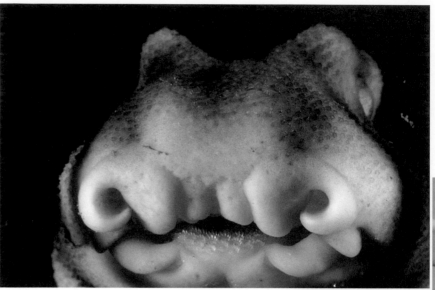

Touch

The sense of touch is the least understood of all the sharks' senses. What we do know is that the senses of touch, temperature detection, and possibly pain detection are localized in sense organs in the skin. Sharks respond to external physical contact, presumably from skin sense organs but also from lateral line and pit organs (see page 58). Sharks also have stretch-reception organs in the skin, known as proprioreceptors, that respond to the movement of skin and muscles. These can be used to fine-tune body movements, particularly those of the fins and jaws, by feeding back information to the brain.

Taste

A shark's sense of taste is localized in specialized clusters of cells (taste buds) on the papillae of the roof and floor of the pharynx and the tongue. Taste is little understood in sharks, but apparently functions when they ingest food and other items. Experiments with free-ranging requiem sharks suggest that they have a well-developed ability to discriminate between tastes. When presented with similar baits from sea bass and certain marine mollusks, the sharks initially took all the baits into their mouths, but consistently spat out the mollusks. Similar experiments with captive requiem sharks suggest that they actively discriminate between the meat of different fishes, spitting out some while avidly consuming others. Apart from its role in food selection, taste may also be involved in detecting differences in salinity in water around the shark.

ABOVE: *A number of senses, including sight, taste, and smell, may have been used by this Caribbean reef shark to catch its prey. Shark senses are complex and intricately integrated.*

RIGHT: *These reef sharks have been attracted by the scent of their prey. While reef sharks head directly up-current toward a scent, some other species prefer to criss-cross the scent path.*

LEFT: *The convoluted nostrils of the hornshark allow water to be pulled by the respiratory current into the nasal cavities, which have large sensory surfaces. Sharks are capable of detecting minute chemical traces with concentrations as low as one part per million.*

SMELL

A shark's sense of smell is localized in paired nasal organs on the underside of its snout. The nostrils lead to blind nasal cavities lined with folds of skin, and sensory cells on these folds are capable of detecting chemicals in water. As a shark swims, water passes into the nasal cavity through the scoop-like, forward-facing nostril openings, passes the sensory folds, and exits through rearward-facing outlets. When sharks are at rest, the respiratory current entering the mouth tends to draw a stream of water into the nostrils. Some bottom-dwelling sharks have developed nasal grooves connecting the nasal outlets with the mouth, and use the respiratory current to actively suck water into the nostrils.

Sharks are renowned for their olfactory acuity. Although most sharks have large to

huge olfactory organs, and presumably have a highly developed sense of smell, few species have been studied in any detail. Experiments with inshore lemon and nurse sharks indicate that they may react to the chemical components of meat and blood (such as amino acids) in concentrations as low as one part per million, which suggests this sense is important for locating and tracking prey. These sharks also react to other chemicals, including ordinary sea salts, suggesting a role in navigation and habitat selection. The response to stimulating chemicals is temporary and the chemicals are quickly flushed out of the nasal cavities.

Sharks are able to determine the direction of an attractive scent in water, and free-ranging pelagic sharks have been repeatedly observed following scent trails up-current to baits or other chemical stimuli. The maximum distance over which sharks can track a scent is difficult to establish, but it is likely to be many miles.

More research is needed into other aspects of the sharks' sense of smell, including the possibility that chemical stimuli are involved in social interactions. Some chemicals are clearly offensive to sharks, and much research has been devoted to the possible application of these chemicals as shark repellents. To date, however, the success of such research has been limited.

SIGHT

All sharks have well-developed eyes that are positioned on the sides of the head, providing a wide field of vision. The smallest eyes occur in reef carpetsharks and some requiem sharks that live in turbid estuaries and rivers, while the largest are found in deep-water dogfish and various lamnoid sharks, such as the bigeye thresher. The basic structure of a shark's eye—cornea, iris, pupil, lens, and retina—is broadly similar to that of other vertebrates.

Sharks that swim near the surface tend to have retinas with numerous cone cells, enabling color vision and visual acuity in daylight. Most species also have mechanisms for regulating the amount of light reaching the retina.

Adaptations to low-light conditions are many and varied. Some species have numerous rod

ABOVE: Shark rattles such as this one have been used for centuries by fishermen on the Solomon Islands to attract sharks. The rattles, which produce low-frequency sounds underwater that are apparently attractive to sharks, were probably developed by trial and error.

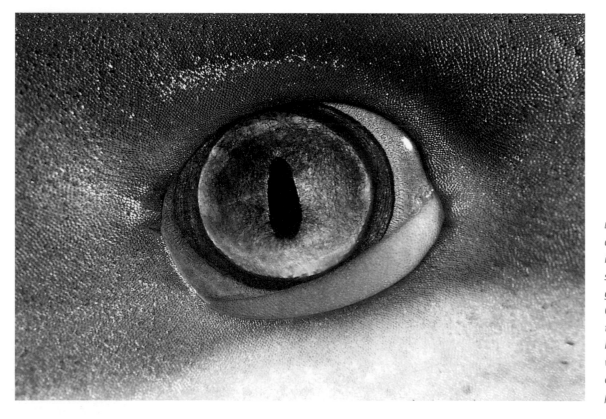

LEFT: The eyes of most sharks are contained within immovable eyelids. However some sharks, particularly ground sharks such as this Galapagos shark, have a tough moveable membrane known as a nictitating eyelid, which rises from the bottom of the eye during feeding to protect the eye from damage.

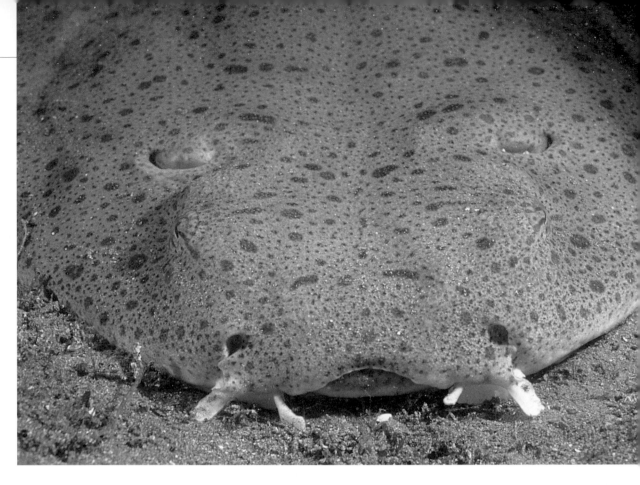

cells in their retinas, allowing them to see and detect movements in low light. Another common adaptation, found also in many nocturnal terrestrial animals, is a reflective layer (tapetum) behind the retina that causes the eye to glow. Sharks that inhabit deep water, where it is inky black but for the light emitted by living organisms, have huge, glowing, green or yellow eyes with large pupils.

Vision may be important for hunting and social interactions in many sharks, but it is a relatively short-ranged sense due to the composition and light-absorbing properties of sea water. Observations of captive lemon sharks suggest that when finding baits, sight may be less important than smell over distances greater than 50 feet (15 m) but more important at distances of less than 10 feet (3 m).

HEARING

As with other vertebrates, the sense of hearing in sharks is localized in the paired inner ears. These are buried inside the braincase and lie alongside the rear of the brain. The inner ears are also a shark's principal organs of balance and coordination. The inner ear detects low-frequency compression waves (sound) in water and regulates balance by detecting the motion

of fluid within its cavities. Inner ears can also detect the pull of gravity and changes in velocity and direction as the shark swims, and may contribute to maintenance of muscle tone.

The inner ears of some inshore sharks are apparently sensitive to compression waves in the water at much lower frequencies than the air-adapted human ear can detect. These sharks can detect sounds of approximately 10 to 800 hertz (cycles per second), while human ears range from about 25 to 16,000 hertz. Over what distance the sense of hearing in sharks operates is unclear, but as water is a good conductor of sound, it may operate over several miles.

Hearing in sharks is apparently directional, which may help them find struggling or injured fishes that are emitting sounds, or potential prey that have natural sound-producing organs. Hearing may also serve in social interactions (as with tail cracking in white sharks) and in helping sharks to avoid sound-producing predators. In various field experiments, large sharks (mostly requiem sharks) were attracted to pulsed, low-frequency sounds produced by underwater loudspeakers over distances of several miles. When certain sounds were produced by the loudspeaker, nearby sharks fled, suggesting that some sounds can also repel sharks.

MECHANOSENSE AND ELECTROSENSE

In addition to the five senses familiar to us (see pages 54–57), sharks have other senses that are difficult for us to imagine, but which are vital for perceiving their world. These include senses for the detection of weak vibrations in the water (mechanosense) and the detection of weak electric fields (electrosense).

THE LATERAL LINE

The lateral line is a pair of sensory tubes that extends beneath the skin from the head to the base of the caudal fin, along the flanks and tail. On the head, the lateral line extends over the eyes, across the top of the head, below the eyes, on the cheeks, and on the snout. The main tubes have pores, or smaller tubes, connecting them to the exterior surface of the skin, although in some primitive deep-water sharks the tubes open to the exterior through a broad groove. Inside the tubes are sets of sensory cells with hair-like protrusions (known as hair cells or neuromasts) that react when the hairs are stimulated by movement and pressure.

Closely related to the lateral line system, but lacking internal tubes, are the pit organs. These are blind pockets in the skin with sensory hair cells inside them. They are scattered over the body and guarded by pairs of denticles.

PICKING UP VIBRATIONS

The lateral line and pit organs are highly sensitive to minute vibrations or displacements of water, and their function is closely related to that of the inner ear (see page 57). The positioning of the lateral line and pit organ systems allows sharks to detect water vibrations (caused by the movement of water molecules) and determine the direction of their source. These vibrations may be produced by the movements of water masses, the shark's own swimming motions, or by the movements of other organisms. The lateral line sense is able to perceive the interplay of water masses and fixed objects, and can be used to detect both predators and prey. It can even detect the respiratory currents of animals buried on the bottom, and may also play a role in social interactions. Over what distance this system operates is unclear, but as with hearing, it may be effective over long distances.

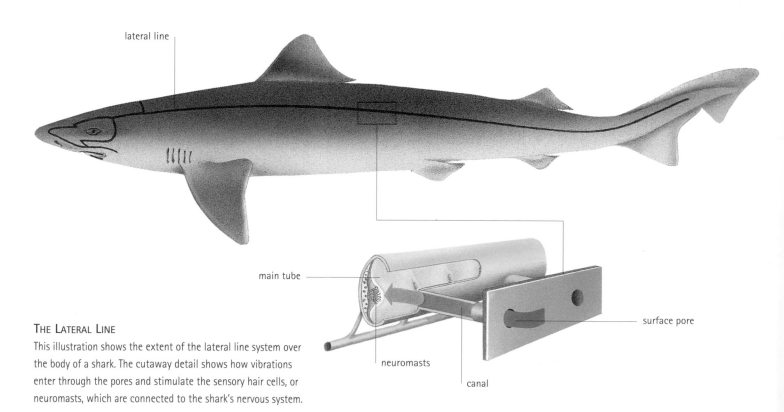

lateral line

main tube

neuromasts

canal

surface pore

THE LATERAL LINE

This illustration shows the extent of the lateral line system over the body of a shark. The cutaway detail shows how vibrations enter through the pores and stimulate the sensory hair cells, or neuromasts, which are connected to the shark's nervous system.

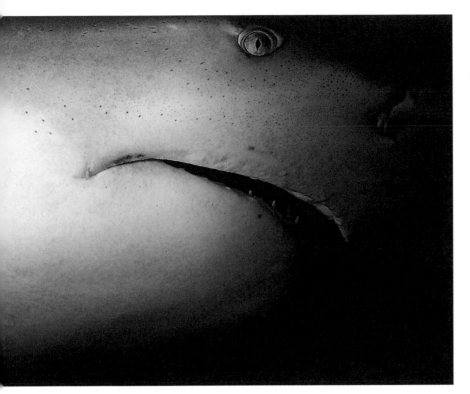

Ampullary organs probably have a number of functions. Early experiments suggested that they are temperature and salinity receptors, or pressure detectors that respond to mechanical stimuli. However, it was also noted that catsharks react to metallic rods but not glass ones, which suggests a sensitivity to electric currents. This was confirmed by severing the nerves to a shark's ampullae. Once the ampullae were disabled, the shark was no longer sensitive to electrical currents

More recently, A.J. Kalmijn, who was also involved in the earlier experiments, demonstrated that the ampullary organs of sharks are sensitive to weak electrical fields produced by the nerves and muscles of other animals. In a series of simple yet elegant experiments, catsharks were able to detect and react to prey fishes that were concealed from their other senses. When these fishes were mimicked by electrodes that produced similar weak electric fields, the catsharks also reacted.

RIGHT: In this close-up of the snout of an Atlantic lemon shark, its ampullae of Lorenzini are clearly visible as large, dark pores. These sensitive electrosense organs are named after Stefano Lorenzini, the Italian anatomist who first described them in 1678. It took another 270 years before scientists began to unravel the secrets of these mysterious organs.

AMPULLAE OF LORENZINI: ELECTROSENSE

Sharks are sensitive to weak electric fields, and this electrosense is localized in specialized sense organs in their heads—the ampullae of Lorenzini. These are located in groups below the skin of the snout, lips, and just behind the eyes. The actual ampullae are sense organs that contain receptor cells in a cluster of open cavities or pockets. These have a common connection to jelly-filled, elongated tubes that extend to pores on the skin's surface. Together the ampullae, tubes, and pores are termed ampullary organs.

The pores form discrete patches on the head, distinct from the lateral line canals, and these can be very large and prominent in large, active pelagic sharks as well as many deep-water sharks. Some sharks have elongated snouts in front of their nostrils, and the spaces between the cartilages that support such snouts are largely occupied by ampullary organs. The greatly swollen and elongated snouts of the deep-water goblin shark and demon catshark are filled with ampullary organs, and their electrosense may be very important in coping with their cold, dark world.

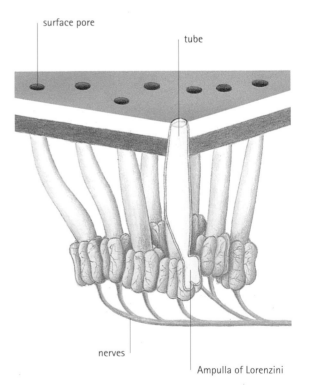

surface pore

tube

nerves

Ampulla of Lorenzini

AMPULLARY ORGANS

Connected to nerves, each ampulla of Lorenzini contains a cluster of sensory cells with a common jelly-filled tube extending to the surface of the shark's skin.

A similar sensitivity to electric fields has been observed in the wild. In another series of experiments, Kalmijn and a colleague used electrodes to attract dusky smoothhounds in waters off Cape Cod, Massachusetts. When electrodes that did not emit an electrical signal were used, the sharks ignored them. It has also been observed that white sharks often investigate metallic objects, such as outboard motors and shark cages, probably because they give off weak electric fields in sea water.

While a shark's electrosense may be able to pick up powerful artificial electrical sources over some distance, it only appears capable of locating biological electrical fields close to the shark's head. Furthermore, the electrosense presumably functions in coordination with

other close-in senses to precisely locate live prey. Observations of scalloped hammerheads hunting and catching buried fish in sand suggest that the electrosense is involved in this feeding behavior, although scent and the lateral line sense may also be involved.

The electrosense may also play a role in the social coordination of some sharks and rays. Certain species of ray have electric organs in their pectoral fins or tails, and many skates produce weak electrical discharges. It is possible that such electrical sources could be readily detected by their own electrosense, and might serve in social communication as well as for defense.

AN ELECTROMAGNETIC COMPASS?
The realization that sharks and the other cartilaginous fishes have an electrosense opened up the possibility that sharks may use this sense to navigate. We know that the earth generates a magnetic field as it rotates, with a north-south

ABOVE: These reef sharks are clearly searching for food, but exactly what combination of senses they are using to find it is difficult to say. The electrosense is one powerful tool at their disposal, but it probably works most effectively in combination with various other senses.

LEFT: One explanation for the tendency of white sharks to investigate shark cages is that these metal cages emit a weak electric field, which is picked up by the shark's acute electrosense.

magnetic polarity. We also know that swimming through this field induces weak electric fields in a shark, and that these fields differ according to the direction the shark is taking relative to magnetic north and south. As these induced fields are within the detection range of a shark's electrosense, couldn't sharks use the differences in the fields as compass bearings?

To test this hypothesis, experiments were conducted with sharks using artificial magnetic fields that could be rotated. These experiments showed that sharks and rays react to changes in the direction of these fields, realigning themselves accordingly. If the artificial magnetic field was so oriented as to cancel out the earth's magnetic field, the animals became disoriented and milled about. Hence it can be assumed that their electrosense functions as an electromagnetic compass, providing positional cues in the absence of external reference points. Similarly, sharks may also be able to use their electrosense to detect the electric fields generated by ocean currents as they move in the earth's magnetic field, and even magnetic differences in bottom topography.

The sensitivity and flexibility of the sharks' electrosense give us a glimpse of how superbly adapted these fishes are to their environment. Just because sharks have been around for a long time, does not mean they are primitive. In fact, the opposite is true. Their long evolutionary history has allowed them to develop unique ways of dealing with their underwater world.

BELOW: The whale shark is a wide-ranging species found in all the oceans of the world. The ability of sharks to navigate over long distances has been attributed to the coordination of their powerful electrosense with the earth's magnetic field.

HOW INTELLIGENT ARE SHARKS?

While some researchers now recognize that complex behavior and potential intelligence exist in sharks, the question of shark intelligence has not had high priority in the annals of shark research. That said, there are major problems involved in studying the intelligence of sharks that extend far beyond the difficulties of working with them in the wild or in captivity.

We tend to define intelligence with reference to our own behavior. However, sharks are very different animals from human beings. They have a long, separate evolutionary history and live in a largely alien sensory world. It is far easier for us to devise psychological tests for laboratory rats or higher primates that share with humans a more recent common ancestry, anatomy, and perception of the world.

ASSESSING SHARK INTELLIGENCE

People often think of sharks as simple-minded "eating machines." However, this is belied by the available evidence. Presumably sharks are less intelligent than highly evolved mammals, if only by comparison of relative and absolute brain size. However, compared to many other animals they have large brains, as well as varied and sophisticated senses. Furthermore, sharks have demonstrated long-term success in coping with a variety of predators and prey, including marine mammals with very large brains.

From a human perspective, measures of intelligence include the complexity, versatility, and malleability of an animal's behavior, and the degree to which learning derives from its parents, society, and environment rather than through innate mechanisms. Unfortunately,

BELOW: The tendency of large requiem sharks, such as these blue sharks, to mill around fishing boats, suggests that these sharks have learned to associate the boats with food scraps thrown overboard.

ABOVE: *Newborn sharks, such as this lemon shark, are born fully formed and survive with little, if any, parental input. However, scientists believe that social interactions with, and learning from, associated newborn sharks are possible.*

RIGHT: *Nurse sharks survive well in captivity, and like the lemon shark, they have been used for learning experiments. Nurse sharks have been shown to be sensitive to minute concentrations of chemicals in the water, which has raised the tantalizing possibility that their sense of smell may be used in social interactions.*

it is difficult to approach the intelligence of sharks from this perspective, as neither innate or learned behavior have been studied in detail.

LEARNING

The little work done on shark learning has focused on lemon and nurse sharks. This work suggests that these sharks readily habituate to captivity, and will react to human observers and to induced stimuli. Experiments show that lemon sharks can learn to perform actions, such as choosing one of a number of options for a food reward. Furthermore, they can remember the correct choice over long periods of time.

Observations of sharks in the wild suggest that certain species are able to learn where and when food will be available, and migrate accordingly (see page 69). Similarly, many large requiem and mackerel sharks follow fishing boats in apparent anticipation of discarded scraps. To what extent these behaviors constitute learning remains open to debate, but many researchers believe the evidence is compelling.

Surprisingly, one shark that is potentially suitable for learning experiments in the wild is the large and formidable great white shark. This is because of its inquisitiveness, quick reaction to stimuli, complex observed behavior, willingness to interact with observers, and ready acceptance of food rewards.

SOCIAL BEHAVIOR AND COMMUNICATION

Shark behavior is poorly known, and this includes their social interactions. A study of the bonnethead shark in captivity suggested that its observable behavior is complex and that much of it has a social context. However, the study did not reveal the developmental basis of the recorded behavior, only its existence.

We do know that sharks can communicate, socially and asocially, with other vertebrates. However, this has been observed in only a few species. Sharks have sensitive hearing in the lower frequencies but the social context of acoustics is little known and sharks are not equipped with specialized sound generators as are many bony fishes. Observations of large requiem sharks reveal that they react to sounds underwater, can associate sounds with food, and may gather when sounds are produced. Tail cracking by white sharks is one possible example of auditory social communication.

Visual displays are known for various requiem and mackerel sharks, the best known being the agonistic display of reef sharks (see page 75). Chemical communication is poorly understood but may by of enormous importance to sharks given their olfactory acuity. Clearly sharks use olfactory cues to find prey, but the role of scent in social interactions remains unclear.

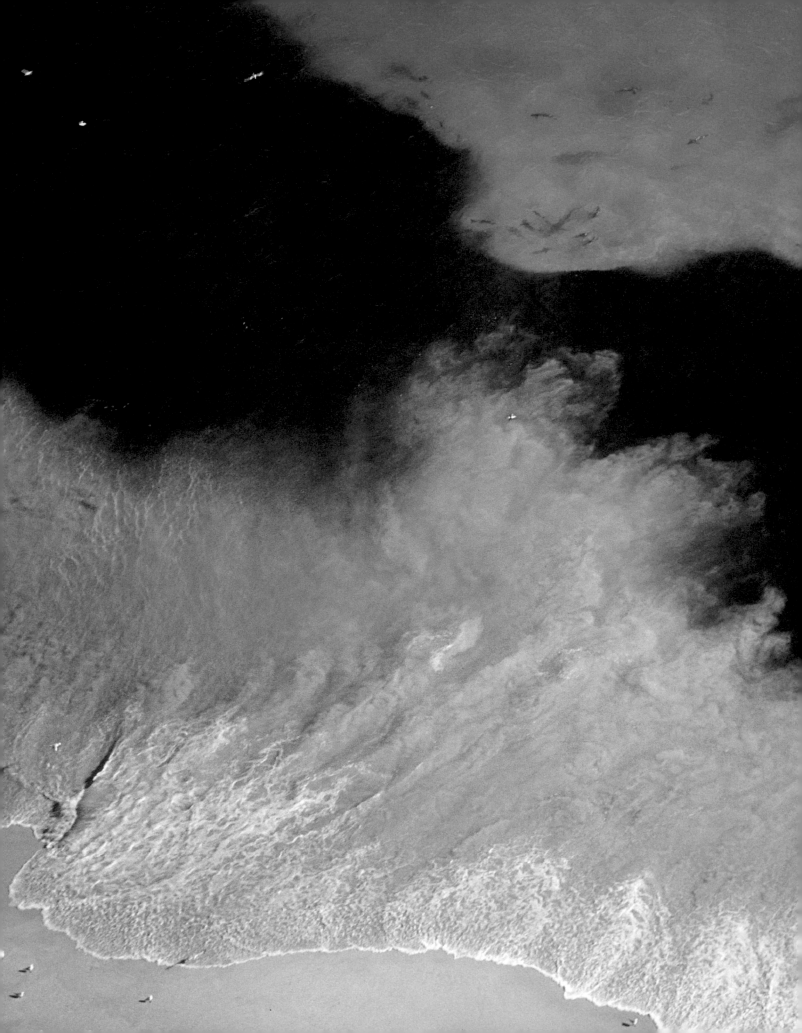

SHARK
BEHAVIOR

Despite a quiet revolution in the study
of sharks in recent years, their world
remains largely shrouded in mystery.
This chapter explores what little
information we have managed to
gather about the behavior of sharks—
how they feed, attack, defend
themselves, socially interact, mate,
reproduce, develop, and migrate.

FEEDING

Sharks have often been portrayed as ferocious ocean predators, the "garbage cans of the sea," feeding continuously and consuming whatever they wish. Although few species have been studied in detail, the reality appears quite different. Sharks eat only what they need in order to survive, grow, and reproduce. They feed, on average, once or twice a week but may go without food for months at a time.

THE SHARKS' DIET

Sharks are carnivores and consume a wide variety of food, ranging from microscopic zooplankton to whales. Active hunting sharks feed mostly on bony fishes, cephalopods, and

LEFT: The basking shark is a filter feeder, straining plankton out of water that passes across its gill arches. These are clearly visible here.

BELOW: The whale shark is another filter feeder, although its diet is more diverse and includes small fishes. However, as the large mouth of the shark can provide cover from other predators, entering it is a risk many fishes are willing to take.

ABOVE: Many bottom-feeding sharks, such as this nurse shark, have powerful jaws and crushing teeth, enabling them to feed on crustaceans, including lobster, as well as mollusks and echinoderms.

RIGHT: Most sharks avoid eating carrion, preferring to feed on live prey. It is only species such as the great white shark or the tiger shark, shown here feeding on a whale carcass in waters off Hawaii, that have the broad cutting teeth necessary to bite chunks of flesh from such large carcasses.

crustaceans. Large active sharks may also eat rays, turtles, dolphins, dugongs, seals, and even other sharks. Some sharks, including smaller bottom dwellers, hunt on the seabed for invertebrates, such as crustaceans, worms, mollusks, and echinoderms.

While most species of shark consume a variety of prey, allowing them to maintain their food intake as the abundance of individual prey changes, some species have very specialized diets. The whiskery shark, for example, which lives around the rocky reefs of southern Australia, feeds almost exclusively on octopus.

The diet of sharks may also change as they mature. Young sandbar sharks found in the shallow bays and coastal waters of eastern North America primarily eat blue crabs, whereas the adults that occur farther offshore prey on fishes and skates.

The tiger shark is probably the only species of shark that deserves its reputation as garbage can of the sea. Tiger sharks are opportunistic feeders eating fishes, sharks, rays, crabs, lobsters, squid, conches, sea birds, sea snakes, turtles, dolphins, dugongs, and whales. They have also been reported to consume terrestrial animals

washed down flooded rivers, such as cows and kangaroos. Researchers studying this species have not only reported a diverse range of animals in their stomachs, but also a bewildering array of garbage, including plastic bags, aluminum foil, wire, lumps of coal, wood, leather, fabrics, tins of food, wallets, and, in one case, a native drum.

LOCATING AND CAPTURING PREY

Sharks use many of their senses to find and capture their prey and are able to detect healthy, wounded, dying, or dead fish over long distances. It is presumed that they are able to home in on scent trails provided by healthy animals, from mucus or other chemicals they emit. Odors from dead or bleeding animals travel many miles on ocean currents and sharks follow these trails until they locate their prey. In experiments conducted by Albert Tester during the late 1950s and early 1960s at the Marine Biology Laboratory at Enewetak Atoll in the Marshall Islands, the activity level of captive blacktip sharks increased dramatically when water in which a fish had been killed was added to the enclosure.

Wounded fishes send out distinctive low-frequency sounds that sharks can home in on. Experiments carried out in the Pacific Islands in the 1960s and 1970s by Arthur Myrburg of the University of Miami, show that sharks can be attracted by playing recordings of struggling fishes and low-frequency pulses underwater.

Vision can play an important role once sharks are within approximately 65 feet (20 m) of their

LEFT: Wobbegong sharks are effective ambush predators. They have tassels around the head and mouth and mottled coloration, making it difficult for potential prey to spot them in their preferred habitat of rocks and seaweed.

prey. Most sharks approach, chase, and attack their prey on the basis of what they can see. In the last split-seconds as the shark lunges at its prey, touch, taste, and the electrical sense (see pages 58–61) probably also play a role.

For some species of shark, their acute electrical and olfactory senses play a primary role in locating prey. Small hammerheads have been observed sweeping their heads back and forth across the ocean floor in search of small fishes hidden there. The sharks can detect the odors of the fishes as well as locate the electrical impulses they emit from their muscles. Once the prey are located, the sharks use their spade-like heads to dislodge and consume them. The epaulette shark, a small species that lives on coral reefs, locates its prey in a similar way. However, instead of digging the prey out, the shark plunges its head into the sand to capture it.

DISABLING PREY
Sharks will often disable their prey before consuming it. In 1988, Rocky Strong from the Costeau Society observed a large hammerhead

shark chasing a stingray in the waters off the Bimini Islands in the Bahamas. Approaching its prey, the shark used the front of its head to push the stingray onto the ocean floor. Holding the stingray down with its head, the shark bit a chunk out of its flap, partially disabling it. The shark then released the stingray only to repeat the process on the other side, disabling it totally.

White sharks feeding on sea lions around the Farallon Islands off the coast of California have also been observed to disable their prey. A shark will bite a seal lion then wait until it dies from the massive wound before consuming it. It is believed that by doing this the white shark reduces the risk of being injured by these large, aggressive animals.

NON-PURSUIT METHODS
Well-camouflaged sharks, such as wobbegongs and angelsharks, lie motionless on the ocean floor waiting in ambush for prey to approach. When a fish ventures too close, the shark will rapidly open its mouth, drawing in water and the prey. The water is then expelled through

ABOVE: Sea lions are often seen bearing the scars of a close encounter with a large shark. The underwater agility of these marine mammals means that, at times, they can escape from an attacking shark, even after being bitten.

the gill openings, and strong, backward-facing, needle-like teeth trap the prey in the shark's mouth before it is consumed whole.

Whale and basking sharks are filter feeders, concentrating on swarms of plankton. They do not use their teeth to capture prey—their gills have long, thin extensions (gill rakers) that form a fine mesh to filter plankton from the water. Whale sharks may swim vertically through these swarms until they reach the surface forcing the plankton-rich water to flow over their gills.

LEARNING WHERE TO LOOK

Evidence suggests that sharks can learn and remember where to find food. Every fall, whale sharks appear off Western Australia's Ningaloo Reef to coincide with the mass spawning of coral and other reef animals, which generates an explosion in the number of plankton. Similarly, tiger sharks enter the waters around the French Frigate Shoals off the northwest Hawaiian Islands every year as young black-footed albatrosses learn to fly. Birds that crash into the ocean are quickly attacked and eaten by the sharks. Sharks have also learned to take advantage of the habits of humans, with many sharks regularly following fishing boats, waiting for old bait or unwanted fishes to be discarded.

FOOD REQUIREMENTS OF SHARKS

The energy requirements of sharks vary significantly between species. Captive bull sharks and blue sharks on average consume 0.5 percent and 0.6 percent respectively of their body weight per day. The mako shark, on the other hand, has the highest energy requirements on account of its active nature and high body temperature, consuming 3.1 percent of its body weight per day. Juvenile sharks also have high food intakes to support rapid growth rates. Newborn sandbar sharks, for example, consume around 1.4 percent of body weight per day, whereas adults eat around 0.9 percent.

Water temperature can also influence the amount that a shark eats. Barry Jones and Glen Geen, of the Simon Fraser University in Vancouver, observed that spiny dogfish in the waters off British Columbia consume twice as much food in summer as they do in winter, when their physiology slows with the decrease in water temperature.

To obtain their energy requirements sharks do not need to feed daily. A shark's stomach will hold around 10 percent of its body weight, so if large prey is consumed, a shark may only need to feed once or twice a week.

RIGHT: *To protect their eyes while feeding, many species of shark, including this oceanic whitetip, have tough nictitating membranes, or eyelids. As the mouth opens to consume the prey, the membrane closes from bottom to top, covering the eye.*

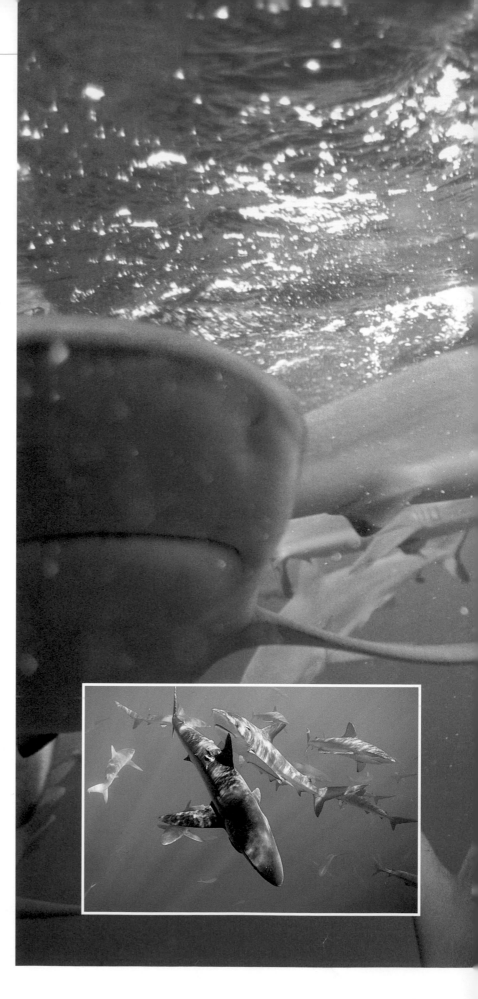

Sharks that consume small prey, such as the brown banded catshark that preys on worms and small crustaceans, need to feed more regularly to meet their energy requirements, possibly as often as twice a day.

Sharks are able to survive for extended periods without feeding by storing energy in their liver as fats and oils. Although normally only required to sustain sharks for periods of a few weeks, these energy reserves can be large enough for some sharks to survive much longer. The basking shark, for example, periodically sheds its gill rakers and is unable to provide for itself during the four to five months it takes for new gill rakers to grow. Amazingly, relatively inactive bottom-dwelling species, such as swellsharks and hornsharks, have survived in captivity for over a year without eating.

"FEEDING FRENZIES"

A common image on television, and one that appears to confirm many people's fears and prejudices regarding sharks, is the "feeding frenzy"—a pack of agitated sharks ripping into baits and sometimes even each other. Such feeding frenzies, however, are actually rare in the wild and are usually the result of humans deliberately overloading the sharks' sensory systems by filling the water with blood and the odors of dead fishes.

While feeding frenzies are rare without human involvement, at times large schools of fish may attract the attention of a group of sharks. In June 1993, an enormous school of baitfish was trapped against a cliff off the coast of Western Australia by thousands of sharks, including duskies, sandbars, makos, and threshers, as well as other fishes and whales. For several weeks the sharks continuously plunged through the schools of baitfish, even beaching themselves at the base of the cliffs in their attempts to catch them.

RIGHT: *During a feeding frenzy, the normally well-ordered behavior of sharks breaks down. Competing for a limited amount of food, sharks swim rapidly in all directions, biting at anything that may get in their way, including other sharks.*
INSET: *This bronze whaler shark was accidentally bitten by another shark during a feeding frenzy.*

SOCIAL BEHAVIOR

While our knowledge of shark behavior is poor, it does appear that sharks spend much of their lives as solitary animals, hunting, feeding, and living by themselves. We know for a fact that they do not form family groups and that there is rarely cooperation between individuals. As a result, they exhibit less complex social behaviors than marine animals such as whales and dolphins.

While many sharks appear to spend much of their time alone, some species are known to school. The purpose of these shark schools is subject to speculation as sharks, unlike smaller fishes, do not need to use them to avoid predation, nor do they feed when in schools.

The best known schooling behavior in sharks is that observed in the scalloped hammerhead. In the Gulf of California, off the coast of Mexico, hammerheads have been seen in schools of up to 225 individuals moving around an undersea mountain during the day. At night the sharks disperse into surrounding areas to feed. Similar schooling behavior has been observed in gray reef sharks at Enewetak Atoll in the Marshall Islands, and in lemon sharks at the Bimini Islands in the

BELOW: Schooling is a social behavior of certain species of shark, most notably hammerheads. When a number of sharks swim together, each member of the school remains a set distance from its neighbor and all members move in the same direction.

ABOVE: While some species of shark form schools and even hunt cooperatively, most species, such as this bronze whaler, spend much of their lives alone.

Bahamas, although there are no more than 25 individuals in any of these groups.

No other species of shark is known to school. However, some species, including spiny dogfish, whiskery sharks, blacktip sharks, and juvenile dusky sharks, will occasionally form aggregations. Large numbers of the species will congregate, mostly attracted by food or the need to reproduce or migrate, but there is no coordination in their movements.

When groups of sharks do gather to feed, a distinct social order has been observed, both within species and between species, and even in predominantly solitary species. For example, in the western North Atlantic during the 1950s and 1960s, Stewart Springer from the

United States Fish and Wildlife Service noted that when feeding on schools of fish, silvertip sharks dominate Galapagos sharks, and both dominate blacktip sharks. It is likely that within aggregations other social interactions take place, but they have never been studied.

COOPERATIVE HUNTING

While most sharks hunt alone, cooperative hunting has occasionally been observed in shark populations. Sevengill sharks hunt in packs to capture large fur seals, which, at up to 775 pounds (350 kg), are more than twice the weight of the largest sevengill. By hunting as a group, a pack of sevengills can attack and consume an animal that a lone sevengill could never feasibly overpower. In the late 1980s, Dave Ebert of Rhodes University in South Africa observed a group of sevengill sharks off the coast of Namibia forming a loose circle around a fur seal. The sharks gradually moved inward, tightening the circle to prevent the seal from escaping. Eventually one of the sharks attacked the seal, signaling for the remaining sharks to start feeding.

Cooperative hunting has not been studied in any other species of shark. However, anecdotal evidence suggests that it may also occur in oceanic whitetips, thresher sharks, sand tigers, and blacktip reef sharks.

POPULATION SEGREGATION

Shark populations are often organized so that animals of the same sex or size live in distinct parts of a species' range. In the waters off Trinidad, for example, adult female golden hammerheads occur in depths from 30 to 60 feet (9 to 18 m), adult males and large juveniles of both sexes occur in depths from 90 to 120 feet (27 to 36 m), and newborn pups live close to shore in depths of less than 30 feet (9 m). It is believed that population segregation may help reduce cannibalism, which could occur when sharks of different sizes interact, or may merely relate to different feeding preferences among the sharks of different age and sex. Whatever the reason, segregation of males and females breaks down during the mating season to allow for reproduction.

RIGHT: Schooling is not the only aggregating behavior of sharks; less-organized groups are commonplace. Here, nurse sharks rest on the ocean floor in a group. The function and significance of this behavior is unknown.

DEFENSE STRATEGIES

Sharks, like nearly every other animal, must defend themselves against predation. It may seem odd to consider the defensive strategies of sharks, but it should be remembered that most sharks are small and vulnerable to predation.

Although the majority of sharks' predators are other sharks, other predators have also been reported. A large groper, for example, has been observed eating a whitetip reef shark, and recently a killer whale was filmed attacking and killing a great white shark near the Farallon Islands, off the coast of California.

AGGRESSION—A FORM OF DEFENSE

Many of the larger, more active sharks use aggression as a form of defense. While this sometimes means that one shark will attack another, it is more common that a shark will first signal its aggressive intentions in order to avoid a physical attack. The best known aggressive (agonistic) display in sharks was first observed in gray reef sharks in the Marshall Islands by Don Nelson of the California State University. Before attacking, the shark displayed its intention by swimming in an exaggerated fashion with its back arched and pectoral fins lowered (see box). This posturing was observed in response to the threatening behavior of other sharks, humans, and even a submersible. If the threatening object backed off, the shark would not attack. If the threat persisted, however, an attack was almost inevitable.

Sharks may also display aggression by "tail cracking." This behavior has been reported in sand tiger sharks in the waters off New South Wales, Australia. A shark will swim directly at an animal posing a threat, and then at the last moment suddenly turn away. As the shark turns, it flicks its tail causing a loud crack, which may startle potential predators.

PHYSICAL DEFENSES

Some species of shark have physical means of defending themselves. Species such as deep-water dogfish sharks and hornsharks have hard, pointed spines in front of their dorsal fins. These spines make it difficult for a predator to consume the shark without injuring its mouth. Rocky Strong of the University of California

observed that large angelsharks will expel hornsharks after grabbing them, possibly because of their fin spines.

One unusual defensive mechanism is that employed by the swellshark. These sharks can greatly increase the size of their body by swallowing water when threatened, making them much more difficult to attack.

CAMOUFLAGE

Camouflage is an effective form of defense for many species of shark. The mottled coloration of wobbegong sharks and the weed-like tassels that surround their mouths make them very difficult to see as they rest in their reef habitat. Many other benthic sharks also have striped, spotted, or blotchy skin patterns to provide camouflage. The newborn young of some species, such as tiger sharks, zebra sharks, gray carpetsharks, and whiskery sharks, have vivid stripes or blotches that eventually fade as they mature. These markings

ABOVE: Whitetip reef sharks often rest by day in caves or under ledges, which provides them with maximum protection when they would be most visible to predators. Once night falls, these sharks become predators themselves, swimming off to hunt alone.

RIGHT: The swellshark has a bizarre defense strategy. It inflates itself to more than twice its usual size, as seen here. By swelling up it appears more threatening than it really is and can wedge itself in narrow crevices, making it difficult for a predator to dislodge.

provide maximum camouflage when sharks are young and most vulnerable to predation.

Sharks that spend most, or all, of their life swimming often have coloration that reduces their visibility in the water. In these species, the underside is lightly colored so that when viewed from beneath the sharks blend with the bright sunlit water. On the upper side these sharks are darker so that when viewed from above they are difficult to distinguish from the ocean around them. Perhaps the most striking color pattern of this nature is that of the mako, a species found in the open ocean. These sharks are vivid blue on the upper surface and sides and white underneath.

OTHER BEHAVIORAL DEFENSES

Some sharks defend themselves by more passive means, such as avoidance. Whitetip reef sharks, a small to medium-sized species that lives on coral reefs in the Indo-West Pacific, appear to defend themselves by remaining mostly inactive during daylight hours. They rest in caves and under ledges, where they are less likely to encounter predators. However, at night they become active, feeding aggressively on reef fishes and invertebrates. Feeding at night is a popular defensive strategy among sharks, and it has been noted that feeding activity increases on nights when there is no moonlight.

WARNING SIGNS

The following series of illustrations compares the threatening display of gray reef sharks (top) with their normal non-threatening behavior (bottom). Researchers believe that this agonistic display is meant as a warning and will only precede an attack if the perceived threat does not retreat.

side view

front view

top view

MATING

Mating has been observed in only a few species of shark, such as the chain catshark, spiny dogfish, smallspotted catshark, and whitetip reef shark. As a result we know very little about reproductive behavior and the reproduction process, despite its importance. However, one thing we do know for certain is that all sharks fertilize their eggs internally, requiring males and females to mate.

CHOOSING A MATE

Compared with other fishes, sharks produce a tiny number of offspring. To ensure that these offspring have the best possible chance of survival, females try to mate with only the healthiest, fittest males. To achieve this, sharks frequently undertake long and, from a human perspective, often very violent and dangerous pre-mating rituals.

It is thought that female sharks secrete chemicals enabling male sharks to sense when they are ready to mate. In those few species where mating behavior has been observed, one or more males follow the female, biting at her back and fins. Competing male whitetip reef sharks become aggressive toward each other as they vie for the right to mate with the female. In the chain catshark, a small egg-laying species of the northwestern Atlantic, the pre-mating ritual lasts over an hour and includes biting and coordinated swimming, whereby the male and female swim side-by-side following each other's movements.

HOW SHARKS MATE

All male sharks possess a pair of claspers, located between the pelvic fins on their underside. These claspers are short and soft in juveniles but become elongated and harden as the shark matures. During mating, a clasper is inserted into the female's cloaca and the sperm is transferred.

While all observed matings have occurred on the sea floor, the mating position of sharks varies with body form. In elongate, flexible species, such as the smallspotted catshark common in European waters, the male wraps himself around the female's pelvic region. The males of less flexible species, such as the

ABOVE: Two nurse sharks perform a mating dance in a sand patch in the Bahamas. Such pre-mating rituals can last for more than an hour.

LEFT: A male shark can always be identified by the pair of claspers located between the pelvic fins. This photograph shows the claspers of an immature whale shark at Ningaloo Reef, Australia. As they mature, the claspers will become longer, extending well beyond the rear of the fins.

whitetip reef shark, position themselves alongside the female, holding one of her pectoral fins in their mouths to maintain the correct mating position. One clasper is inserted into the cloaca with the tip being splayed outward to maintain its position. Some species, such as the spiny dogfish, have spines and hooks on the end of the clasper for added anchorage.

Mating can last from about 30 seconds in captive chain dogfish to between 1½ and 4 minutes in captive whitetip reef sharks. The success of mating in some species is low. Observations of nurse sharks mating in Florida found that only 10 percent of matings ended successfully. Part of the reason for this low success rate is that another male may try to muscle in during the mate in an attempt to simultaneously mate with a single female.

FREQUENCY OF MATING

Sharks normally have a single mating season each year that lasts anywhere from a couple of days to several months. It is not known how often males and females mate during each season or with how many partners. Although the mating season occurs annually and mature males mate every season, individual females of some species only mate every second or third season. This occurs because the female either carries her young for more than a year or rests for a year or two between pregnancies. The spiny dogfish, for example, has a gestation period of 22 months making annual breeding impossible, and the dusky and soupfin sharks are thought to rest between pregnancies for one and two years respectively. Some species, such as the Caribbean sharpnose shark, do not mate seasonally; instead they are able to mate at any time during the year.

RIGHT: *Biting is a pre-mating behavior that is common to all observed shark species. Here, a male zebra shark seizes the tail of a female, flipping her onto her back.*

SHARK REPRODUCTION

In sharks, each mating produces a few well-developed young that have a high survival rate. This reproductive strategy is in stark contrast to that of most fish species, which produce millions of tiny eggs, only a fraction of which survive. Sharks provide nutrients and protection to their developing young in a number of ways, from laying eggs to mammal-like placental nutrition to bizarre forms where developing embryos consume their siblings.

OVIPARITY

The simplest form of reproduction, observed in species including hornsharks, catsharks, and epaulette sharks, is that of egg-laying. After fertilization, each egg is enclosed in a tough, flexible case. These egg cases are normally purse-shaped, although hornsharks produce egg cases that are conical and have a broad spiral ridge, giving them a distinctive screw-shaped appearance.

ABOVE: Hornsharks produce unusual cone-shaped egg cases, which are not anchored like the cases of other sharks. Instead they are wedged in crevices and may become dislodged during severe storms, sometimes washing up on beaches.

LEFT: The egg case of the lesser spotted dogfish, like those of all egg-laying sharks, is constructed of protein that toughens after it is formed. This process is known as tanning, and the resulting egg case provides protection from most predators, but remains permeable to water and gases.

Some female sharks lay a pair of eggs at a time, but may then go on to produce several dozen eggs from the same mating over a period of a couple of months to a few years. Chain catsharks held in captivity have laid up to 70 pairs of eggs over a three-year period from a single mating. The egg cases are laid in protected areas or anchored to the ocean floor, seaweed, or the skeletons of benthic animals. Chain catshark egg cases have sticky tendrils projecting from their ends—the female shark winds the tendrils around vertical structures, such as seaweed or coral, as she lays them.

The embryo's only source of nutrition is the large amount of yolk within the egg. As the embryo develops, a seam along one side of the egg case splits, allowing water to flow around the egg. This enables gases and waste to exchange more easily than they would through the thick egg case. To help the circulation of water, the developing shark swims within the case, and when the yolk is exhausted, it hatches through the open seam.

RETAINED OVIPARITY

Retained oviparity, or ovoviviparity, is used by only a small number of shark species. It is a reproductive style similar to oviparity but provides greater protection to the developing embryos. The eggs, which are still encased, are retained within the female's body and never laid. The best known example is that of the whale shark, which carries several hundred eggs that each produces young about 2 feet (60 cm) in length. The young hatch from the eggs inside the mother's body and are born live.

YOLK-SAC VIVIPARITY

This is the most common reproductive method among sharks. As in the case of ovoviviparity, the young are retained in the female's body and the yolk is the major source of nutrients for the developing embryos. However, here the egg case is reduced to a thin membrane surrounding the embryo. In some species, such as the spiny dogfish, this membrane contains a number of eggs.

During development the yolk is stored in a thin-walled yolk sac, which is connected to the embryo by a thin cord. In addition to the yolk, it has been suggested that some species provide nutrients to the embryos by way of secretions from the uterus wall, which pass across the egg membrane. Examples of species that have yolk-sac viviparity include wobbegongs, houndsharks, angelsharks, and sevengill sharks.

ABOVE: Pregnant leopard sharks, such as these in a shallow bay in California, carry their young internally. The developing embryos are nourished by way of a connected yolk sac.

PLACENTAL VIVIPARITY

Some species of shark have developed a system of embryonic nutrition similar to that of most mammals. Species such as the dusky, blue, hammerhead, spadenose, smoothhound, blacktip, and silvertip shark, develop a placenta and umbilical cord that provide a direct link between the mother and embryo for the exchange of nutrients, oxygen, and waste.

The placenta is usually formed a couple of months into development of the embryos. To sustain the embryo prior to placental development, the eggs contain yolk, but much less than for egg-laying or yolk-sac-viviparous species. As the yolk is exhausted, the yolk sac in which the yolk is stored fuses with the wall of the uterus to form the placenta. In the spadenose shark this system is so advanced that the eggs contain very little yolk and the placenta is formed within days.

Some placental species also provide nutrients to the embryos by way of secretions from the uterus. The umbilical cords of sharpnose and hammerhead sharks possess numerous hair-like projections, called appendiculae, that absorb these nutrients, passing them to the embryo to help fuel development.

UTERINE CANNIBALISM

Sharks of the order Lamniformes (including the great white, thresher, sand tiger, mako, and basking sharks), the false catshark, and the slender houndshark have a unique reproductive strategy. Early development of the embryos proceeds like that of other sharks, with the yolk providing nutrition. However, when the embryos reach about 4 inches (10 cm) in

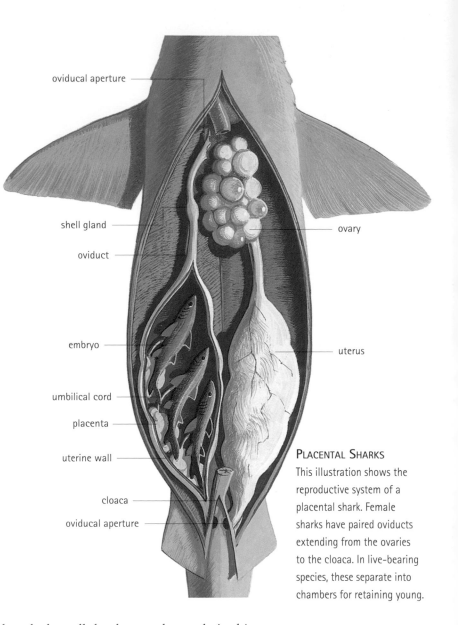

PLACENTAL SHARKS

This illustration shows the reproductive system of a placental shark. Female sharks have paired oviducts extending from the ovaries to the cloaca. In live-bearing species, these separate into chambers for retaining young.

length the yolk has been exhausted. At this point the mouths of the embryos become functional and they begin to consume unfertilized eggs that the mother releases into her uterus, a process known as oophagy. The embryos store the devoured egg yolk in their stomachs, which function much like the yolk sac in yolk-sac-viviparous species.

Sand tiger sharks have taken this form of reproduction to bizarre lengths. Once the yolk in the egg has been exhausted, the embryos start to consume their siblings, rather than the unfertilized eggs. The mouth and teeth of the embryos are well developed to assist in this form of uterine cannibalism, called adelophagy.

LEFT: Many sharks lay eggs in translucent cases in which the embryos develop until they are ready to hatch. Here we see a developing swellshark embryo connected to the large yolk that sustains it. When the yolk is exhausted, the shark will hatch through a split in the egg case.LEFT:

Initially female sand tigers carry up to 40 young in each of their two uterine chambers, but only one survives until birth. After preying on its siblings, the remaining embryo in each chamber is nourished by unfertilized eggs.

GESTATION PERIOD

The gestation period, or time that embryos take to develop within the mother's body, varies considerably between species of shark. Gestation periods of most sharks range from 9 to 12 months. The shortest known gestation period is around five months for the bonnet-head shark and the longest is that of the spiny dogfish—at about 22 months it is the longest known gestation period of any animal.

THE BIRTH

When they are ready to give birth, female live-bearing sharks will often enter special nursery areas. These ensure that the young are safe from predation by larger sharks. Females stop feeding around the time of birth, which provides further protection from predation. Captive sandbar sharks, for example, stop feeding about two weeks prior to pupping.

Prior to birth, females secrete a chemical called relaxin that relaxes their uterus and eases the passage of the young from the body. The young emerge from the female tail first and

upside down, and are immediately able to swim. In placental species the umbilical cord breaks as the young shark is born. Newborn placental and yolk-sac viviparous sharks can be identified by the scar where the umbilical cord joined the body. Observations of captive sandbar sharks have shown that it takes around six minutes for a young shark to emerge from its mother.

The size of young sharks at birth varies enormously between species. The Caribbean lanternshark, a small deep-water species, is about 3½ inches (9 cm) long at birth. Egg-laying sharks are typically 6 to 10 inches (15 to 25 cm) long when they hatch, while live-bearing species have young that are normally between 8 and 40 inches (20 and 100 cm) long. Species that employ uterine cannibalism produce the largest offspring. White, thresher, and sand tiger sharks produce young 48 to 60 inches (120 to 150 cm) long. The basking shark is believed to produce the longest young at around 66 inches (170 cm).

The greatest observed number of offspring carried at one time is 307, by a whale shark harpooned off Taiwan in 1995. The next most prolific producer is the oceanic blue shark, with litters of up to 132 young. Such large litters, however, are unusual; the majority of sharks have between 4 and 20 young each time they reproduce. A few species, such as the little gulper shark, produce only a single pup at a time.

DEVELOPMENT AND GROWTH

As soon as a shark is born, or laid in the form of a cased egg, it is completely independent of its mother. Its body is perfectly formed and all of its senses are functional. Since sharks spend no time at all with their parents, behavior at birth is innate. To help newborn sharks survive until they have become adept at hunting and catching prey, a large amount of energy is stored in their liver.

Sharks are often born in a distinct part of a species range, known as the nursery area. For inshore sharks these are normally located in coastal waters where food is plentiful and temperatures warm, allowing the juveniles to grow rapidly. These areas are avoided by adult sharks, who might otherwise prey on the young. Such predation could threaten the survival of the entire population.

GROWTH RATES

Sharks grow fastest when they are young, reducing the amount of time during which they are most vulnerable to predation. Species that are smallest at birth tend to grow fastest. For example, the smooth dogfish, found in estuaries along the New Jersey coast, are 12 to 16 inches (30 to 40 cm) long at birth and grow approximately ½ inch (2 mm) per day after birth. After six months, when they leave the estuaries for their wintering grounds, they have more than doubled in length.

It is not always small sharks that grow rapidly. The tiger shark, for example, which is born at 20 to 30 inches (50 to 75 cm) and grows to over 20 feet (6.1 m), doubles its length in the first year after birth. Other species, such as the dusky shark, grow at a steadier rate. At birth this species is about 40 inches (100 cm) in length. It grows 4 inches (10 cm) a year as a juvenile, taking around 20 years to reach maturity.

As sharks mature, their reproductive organs enlarge and become functional. A female's ovaries begin to develop yolky eggs that will go on to provide some, if not all, of the nutrition for the embryos. The claspers of the male shark grow in length, and then the supporting cartilages become hardened by calcification to enable mating to occur. A great deal of energy is now required for reproduction, so growth rates slow considerably.

The age of sharks at maturity varies greatly between species. While most species of shark reach maturity at 5 to 10 years of age, small warm-water sharks can mature more rapidly, and others, including cold-water sharks and large sharks, can take much longer. The Australian sharpnose shark, a small species common to the inshore waters of northern Australia, matures within one year of birth, whereas the dusky shark does not fully develop until it is 20 years old or more.

BELOW: This sequence shows a swellshark emerging from its egg case. When sharks emerge they often have distinctive color patterns that provide camouflage, protecting them from predators. As they grow and are less likely to be attacked, the patterns often fade.

ABOVE: Juvenile sharks, such as this one-year-old lemon shark, tend to have much smaller home ranges than adults of the same species. Lemon sharks, which inhabit shallow reef flats near mangroves, have a home range of less than ½ square mile (1 sq km), while adults range over 20 square miles (50 sq km) or more.

LIFESPAN

Similarly, the lifespan of sharks varies dramatically, from only a few years to more than 70 years. Small warm–water sharks have the shortest lives, most living less than 10 years. Bonnethead sharks in the waters off Florida, for example, live for a maximum of six years. Larger species and those that inhabit cooler waters normally live longer. Spiny dogfish, which inhabit cool temperate waters worldwide, live for up to 70 years. A soupfin shark captured off northeastern Tasmania, Australia, in 1951 was recaptured more than 35 years later. It was estimated to be at least 10 years old when first captured, indicating that this species can live for more than 45 years. Although little is known about the lifespan of deep-water sharks, the cool temperature of their environment suggest that they grow slowly and live for a long time.

DETERMINING A SHARK'S AGE

The age of many sharks can be determined by examining their vertebrae. Like trees, the vertebrae of sharks have concentric rings that are laid down on a regular basis. Most sharks produce the bands annually, although some species may produce two or more each year. In dead sharks, the bands can be revealed by staining the vertebrae (see illustration) and then counted to provide an estimate of the shark's age. A shark's age can also be estimated from dorsal fin spines, which also have bands, or by using tagging methods (see pages 144–147).

bands

MIGRATION

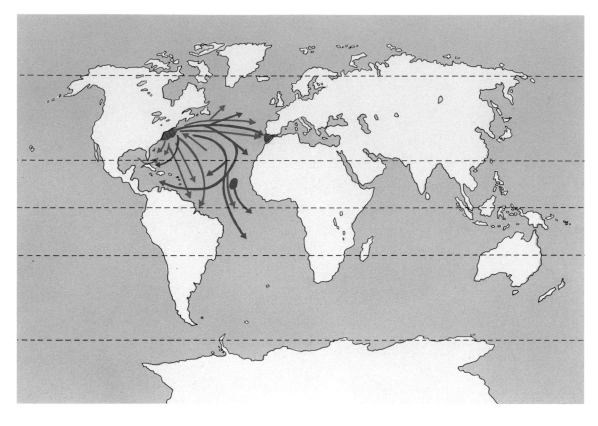

SHARK MIGRATION
Recaptures of blue sharks have shown that this species moves around the Atlantic Ocean following the Gulf Stream current, venturing as far as Brazil, west Africa, and the Mediterranean Sea. Mako sharks migrate individually from the northeast coast of the United States, where they spend the summer months, to their wintering grounds in the warmer waters from the Gulf Stream to the Sargasso Sea.

Map Key

Mako sharks

Blue sharks

M igration, either in groups or individually, is an important part of life for many species of shark. Sharks migrate to find food and to reproduce, and in response to seasonal fluctuations in water temperature. Shark migrations have been studied by releasing tagged sharks and examining the pattern of recaptures or by tracking individual sharks using transmitters (see pages 144–147).

The distance that sharks migrate depends on their swimming ability. While some species, such as the epaulette and gray carpetshark, may not migrate at all, powerful swimming species, such as the mako and blue shark, may cross entire oceans. The longest observed migration was that of a blue shark, tagged in 1983 off the New York coast. It was recaptured 17 months later off the coast of Brazil, an incredible 3,740 miles (6,020 km) away. A number of other species, including the sandbar, dusky, and tiger sharks, have been tagged off the east coast of the United States and observed to cover distances of 1,800 miles (2,900 km). These species, however, confine migration largely to the continental shelf.

WHY DO SHARKS MIGRATE?

Sharks sometimes migrate to take advantage of food sources. Mako sharks migrate onto the continental shelf of the northeastern United States in summer to feed on schools of bluefish that congregate there. Similarly, great white sharks migrate northward along the east and west coasts of Australia following the migration of humpback whales to their summer pupping grounds. The white sharks feed on baby whales that are sick or stray too far from their mothers.

With males and females often occupying different parts of a species' range, sharks may migrate to a mating area for reproduction. When it is time to pup, pregnant females may

LEFT: Tagged sharks have provided most of our information about shark migrations. New technologies such as archival tags, which store the animal's location each day, and satellite tags, which download their location whenever they break the surface, are improving our ability to understand and monitor shark movements.

also migrate to special nursery areas. In southern Australia, the soupfin shark travels more than 1,180 miles (1,900 km) from feeding areas in the Great Australian Bight to estuaries in Victoria and Tasmania to give birth.

Water temperature also plays an important role in controlling migration routes. Many sharks demonstrate a preference for water of consistent temperature throughout the year. So, as water temperatures change with the seasons, these sharks migrate. The dusky shark is found in waters off South Africa where the temperature is around 66°F (19°C). As the water temperature along the coast changes with the seasons, the dusky shark follows the water of its preferred temperature.

WHEN DO SHARKS MIGRATE?

Most sharks migrate annually. Each year during summer many species, including the dusky, sandbar, blacktip, and tiger shark, migrate from the Gulf of Mexico to the east coast of the United States. Once there, they give birth to

their young before migrating south again as winter approaches. They are in turn replaced by spiny dogfish and dusky smoothhounds that migrate from deep water to near the coast. In the waters around western Europe, the spiny dogfish population undertakes annual migrations through the North and Irish seas, and between Scotland and the coast of Norway.

Other migrations are less regular. For example, migration in the sand tiger shark population off the east coast of the United States is often associated with their sex and stage of maturity. The young are born in offshore pupping grounds between Cape Canaveral and Cape Hatteras then migrate to inshore nursery areas between Cape Hatteras and Cape Cod shortly after birth. Juvenile males then migrate south every winter to offshore areas and return northward in summer. Juvenile females, on the other hand, remain in the northern nursery areas until they reach maturity, at which point they migrate southward, remaining south of Cape Hatteras for life.

BELOW: The blue shark, seen here in waters off California, can migrate over great distances with incredible accuracy. Tracking suggests sharks may use anomalies in the earth's magnetic field to gain their bearings.

INSET: Little is known of the migration of small sharks. An exception is the Port Jackson shark, which lives in the waters of southern Australia. Adult females released around Sydney migrate as far as northern Tasmania, over 500 miles (800 km) away.

IDENTIFYING SHARKS

While the differences between many species of shark may be subtle, overall there is an enormous diversity of size, shape, color, distribution, behavior, and methods of reproduction. Here we examine more than 50 shark species, covering at least one member from each of the 34 families.

SHARK ORDERS AND FAMILIES

While there is some disagreement among scientists regarding the classification of sharks, they are generally divided into eight orders. These are further subdivided into families, with a variable number of species in each. The following descriptions are based largely on external features, most of which are illustrated and explained on page 10.

FRILLED AND SIXGILL AND SEVENGILL SHARKS (ORDER HEXANCHIFORMES)

Comprising two families, these sharks have six or seven pairs of gill openings (most sharks have five), an anal fin, and a single, spineless dorsal fin. They are wide ranging and are mostly found in deep water. (See page 96.)

Frilled sharks (family Chlamydoselachidae) have compressed, eel-like bodies. The mouth is at the tip of the snout rather than under the head, and they have teeth with three cusps in both jaws. There are one or two species.

Sixgill and sevengill sharks (family Hexanchidae), also known as cow sharks, have cylindrical bodies, mouths under the head, and large, comb-like teeth in the lower jaw. There are four or five species.

DOGFISH SHARKS (ORDER SQUALIFORMES)

The seven families in this order have two dorsal fins (either spined or spineless), no anal fin, a short to moderately long conical snout, and five pairs of gill openings. Most dogfish occur in deep water on the slopes of continents and islands, but some occur in temperate inshore waters, and a few range as far as the Arctic and Antarctic. (See pages 97–101.)

Bramble sharks (family Echinorhinidae) are large, cylindrical sharks with small, spineless dorsal fins on the back over the pelvic fins. Unlike other dogfish, their denticles are large and tack-like. There are two species.

Dogfish sharks (family Squalidae) are moderate-sized, cylindrical sharks. They have compressed, single-cusped cutting teeth in both jaws; strong, ungrooved dorsal fin spines; and no subterminal notch on the caudal fin. There are 11 species.

Gulper sharks (family Centrophoridae) are moderate-sized, cylindrical sharks with compressed, single-cusped cutting teeth in both jaws; a subterminal notch on the caudal fin; and broad dorsal fins with strong, grooved spines. There are more than 14 species.

Lanternsharks (family Etmopteridae) are small to dwarf, cylindrical sharks with grooved spines on the dorsal fins. They are elusive deep-water sharks, named for their luminous organs. In most of the 45 species the caudal fin has a subterminal notch.

Sleeper sharks (family Somniosidae) are moderate-sized to gigantic, cylindrical sharks.

ABOVE: A school of spiny dogfish (family Squalidae) in waters off Miami. Sharks of the order Squaliformes are characterized by the absence of an anal fin.

LEFT: As the name suggests, the sevengill shark (family Hexanchidae) is immediately recognizable by its seven pairs of external gill slits. The other unusual feature of sharks from this order is the single dorsal fin, situated far back along the body.

They have broad, moderate-sized dorsal fins with or without small grooved spines; a caudal fin, usually with a subterminal notch; and small hooked or flat denticles. There are more than 15 species, including the Greenland shark, which can tolerate frigid polar seas.

Roughsharks (family Oxynotidae) are unusual-looking deep-water sharks. Their bodies are smallish and compressed, giving them an inflated, triangular appearance, and their common name derives from the rough, hooked denticles on their skin. There are five or six species of roughshark, all with a subterminal notch on the caudal fin, and huge, broad dorsal fins with strong spines that are mostly buried within the fins.

Kitefin sharks (family Dalatiidae) are dwarf to moderate-sized, cylindrical or slightly compressed sharks. The broad dorsal fins are either spineless or have a minute first dorsal spine, and the caudal fin has a subterminal notch. The small denticles are usually flat and some species have luminous organs. There are at least nine species, including the cookiecutter shark and one of the world's smallest sharks, the spined pygmy shark.

INSET: This Japanese sawshark (family Pristiophoridae) exhibits the formidable saw-like snout that gives the order its common name.
BELOW: The angelshark (family Squatinidae), seen here in east Australian waters, is a highly flattened bottom dweller, often mistaken for a ray. These sharks were once known as monkfish because their unusual heads resemble a monk's hood.

SAWSHARKS (ORDER PRISTIOPHORIFORMES)

There is one family (Pristiophoridae) of these small to moderate-sized, elongated, flat-headed sharks. Believed to be the closest living relatives of the rays, their most distinctive feature is a long, saw-like snout with two long barbels. They also have two spineless dorsal fins, no anal fin, and five or six pairs of gill openings. There are more than five species, occurring in shallow to deepish water on the shelves and slopes of the western North Atlantic, Indian, and Pacific oceans. (See page 101.)

ANGELSHARKS (ORDER SQUATINIFORMES)

These comprise a single family (Squatinidae) of moderate-sized, highly flattened sharks. While ray-like in appearance, they are only distantly related to the rays. They have two small, spineless dorsal fins; no anal fin; a short, truncated snout with a mouth at the tip; five

pairs of gill openings; and huge pectoral fins with angular extensions covering the gill openings. Most of the more than 15 species occur inshore in temperate waters, with a few found in deep tropical waters. (See page 101.)

HORNSHARKS
(ORDER HETERODONTIFORMES)
Comprising a single family (Heterodontidae), hornsharks are named for the spine on each of their two dorsal fins. Also known as bullhead sharks, they are small and large headed with five pairs of gill openings, two large dorsal fins, an anal fin, and a short, pig-like snout. There are at least eight species, found in the warm continental waters of the Pacific and Indian oceans. (See page 102.)

CARPETSHARKS
(ORDER ORECTOLOBIFORMES)
This order comprises seven families of small to gigantic sharks. They have two spineless dorsal fins, an anal fin, a short mouth in front of the eyes, five pairs of gill openings, and nostrils with barbels. The pectoral fins of many species are specially adapted for "walking" on the sea floor. They are found in warm-temperate and tropical waters, with most species occurring in the Indo-West Pacific. (See pages 103–107.)

There are at least six species of collared carpetshark (family Parascylliidae), all small, narrow headed, long tailed, and slender. They have side grooves on the nostrils and a distinctive band around the head like a necklace. They have an angular anal fin, well in front of the short, low caudal fin. There are no ridges on the body or keels on the tail.

Blind sharks (family Brachaeluridae), so named because they close their eyes when caught by anglers, are small, stocky, broad-headed, long-tailed sharks. They have side grooves on the nostrils and an angular anal fin that is slightly in front of the short, low caudal fin. There are no ridges on the body or keels on the tail. There are two species.

Wobbegongs (family Orectolobidae) are small to large with flat, broad bodies and short tails. They have conspicuous folds of skin on the sides of their heads; large, fang-like front teeth; and an angular anal fin that is slightly in front of the short, low caudal fin. There are no ridges on the body or keels on the tail. Many of the six or more species are superbly camouflaged, most notably the tasselled wobbegong, which has fleshy tassels on its chin and jaw resembling kelp or weed.

There are at least 12 species of longtailed carpetshark (family Hemiscylliidae), divided

RIGHT: There is no mistaking the zebra shark (family Stegostomatidae), seen here in waters off Malaysia. Its tail is low and almost as long as the rest of its body. Juveniles have zebra-like stripes, which gradually fade to the yellow and brown spots seen here.

LEFT: Hornsharks (family Heterodontidae) are instantly recognizable by their pig-like snouts, broad eye ridges, and sharp spines on each dorsal fin. They combine sharp front teeth with blunt back teeth, a configuration suitable for eating both soft-bodied and hard-shelled prey.

RIGHT: *The necklace carpetshark (family Parascylliidae) gets its common name from the dark, white-spotted band around its neck. Its trumpet-shaped nostrils are highly convoluted, suggesting that they play an important role in finding prey on the seabed.*

into the epaulette and bamboo sharks. They are small, slender, narrow-headed, long-tailed sharks with side grooves on the nostrils, and a rounded anal fin just in front of the short, low caudal fin. Some species have ridges on the body but none has keels on the tail.

The single species of zebra shark (family Stegostomatidae) is large, stocky, and broad headed. These sharks have an angular anal fin just in front of the caudal fin, which is low and spectacularly elongated—the tail is almost as long as the rest of the body. There are no side grooves on the nostrils or keels on the tail, but there are prominent ridges on the body.

Nurse sharks (family Ginglymostomatidae) are small to large, stocky, and broad headed. They have an angular anal fin just in front of the short, low caudal fin. There are no side grooves on the nostrils, ridges on the body, or keels on the tail. There are three species.

The single species of whale shark (family Rhincodontidae) is the largest living fish. These sharks are gigantic, broad-headed, filter feeders with very large gill openings and internal filter screens, and an angular anal fin well in front of the high, crescent-shaped caudal fin. They have very small, rasp-like teeth; prominent ridges on the body; and strong keels on the tail.

MACKEREL SHARKS (ORDER LAMNIFORMES)

This order contains seven families of mostly large sharks. They have two spineless dorsal fins, an anal fin, five pairs of gill openings, and a long mouth extending past the eyes. Their eyes do not have nictitating eyelids and their nostrils lack barbels. They occur in all cold to tropical seas, mostly in coastal and oceanic waters. (See pages 106–112.)

Goblin sharks (family Mitsukurinidae) are mysterious deep-water sharks with strange elongated, blade-like snouts. There is only one species of this large, soft-bodied shark.

Sand tiger sharks (family Odontaspididae) are large, stout-bodied sharks with short snouts, narrow gill openings, large dorsal and anal fins, and a short caudal fin with a small lower lobe. There are three or four species.

Crocodile sharks (family Pseudocarchariidae) are small, long, cylindrical sharks with short conical snouts, very large eyes, small fins, caudal keels, and long, dagger-like teeth. There is only one species.

Only discovered in 1976, the single species of megamouth shark (family Megachasmidae) is a very large, deep-water filter feeder. Its huge mouth appears at the end of its very short, broadly rounded snout.

Thresher sharks (family Alopiidae) are large, stout-bodied sharks with large pectoral fins, big eyes, and an enormous caudal fin, which is almost as long as the rest of its body. There are three or four species.

Basking sharks (family Cetorhinidae) are gigantic, stocky filter feeders with enormous gill openings, a conical snout, strong caudal keels, and a short, crescent-shaped caudal fin. They are the second largest fish in the world, after the whale shark. There is only one species.

Mackerel sharks (family Lamnidae) are large to very large, spindle-shaped sharks with very broad gill openings, no gill rakers, strong caudal keels, and a short, crescent-shaped caudal fin. There are five species, including the great white, mako, porbeagle, and salmon shark.

GROUND SHARKS (ORDER CARCHARHINIFORMES)

The eight families of ground shark range from small to very large. They have two spineless dorsal fins, an anal fin, a short mouth in front of the eyes, five pairs of gill openings, nictitating eyelids, and nostrils that usually lack barbels. These are the dominant group of sharks, in terms of abundance and number of species, and are found in most cold to tropical seas as well as in fresh water. (See pages 113–123.)

Catsharks (family Scyliorhinidae) are small, slender sharks and the first dorsal fin is over or behind the pelvic fin (in other families of this order the first dorsal fin is in front of the pelvic fin). This is the largest shark family with more than 102 species, including the swellsharks.

Finback catsharks (family Proscylliidae) are small, slender sharks. They have angular mouths with comb-like teeth at the corners. There are no deep grooves in front of their eyes and no precaudal pits. There are at least five species.

False catsharks (family Pseudotriakidae) are small to large sharks. They have deep grooves in front of their eyes, an angular mouth, comb-like teeth at the mouth corners, and no precaudal pits. There are at least two species.

ABOVE: The mysterious megamouth shark (family Megachasmidae) was only discovered in 1976 when a specimen became entangled in a deep-water net. Since then only nine others have been observed, including this one in waters off California. These huge sharks are believed to be filter feeders and generally inhabit very deep water, hence the infrequency of encounters with humans.

Barbeled houndsharks (family Leptochariidae) are small, tapering sharks with barbels on the nostrils, an arched mouth, and very long labial furrows. The teeth at the corners of the mouth are not comb-like, and there are no precaudal pits. There is only one species.

Houndsharks (family Triakidae) are slender, small to moderately large sharks. They have an arched or angular mouth with teeth at the corners that are not comb-like. There are no precaudal pits and there are generally no barbels on the nostrils. There are more than 36 species, including the soupfin and gummy shark.

Weasel sharks (family Hemigaleidae) are small to moderately large, slender sharks. They have nearly circular eyes and precaudal pits. There are more than seven species.

Requiem sharks (family Carcharhinidae), sometimes referred to as whaler sharks, are a diverse group, ranging from small to very large, and stocky to slender. They have nearly circular eyes and precaudal pits. There are more than 50 species, including reef, blacktip, whitetip, tiger, lemon, and blue sharks.

Hammerhead sharks (family Sphyrnidae) range from small to very large. They are very similar to requiem sharks but for one highly distinctive feature—a hammer-shaped head with eyes situated at the extreme ends. There are at least eight species.

BELOW: An aggregation of Caribbean reef sharks (family Carcharhinidae) in waters off the Bahamas. These large, stout requiem sharks are fast swimmers. They often rest in caves or under ledges during the day, preferring to hunt and feed at night.

HOW TO USE THE SHARK IDENTIFICATION GUIDE

The Identification Guide is a practical introduction to many of the world's most important and interesting shark species. You can use it not only to identify sharks you see in the field, but to learn in advance about many of the different species you are most likely to encounter. Information is included about the habitat and distribution of each species, which is particularly useful if you are planning to dive in an area and want to know what species of shark occur there.

The guide is divided into eight color-coded sections representing the eight orders of shark. At least one species from each of the 35 families

is included, with 51 species covered overall. These include those most likely to be sighted as well as some of the more unusual species. Each entry includes the following features:

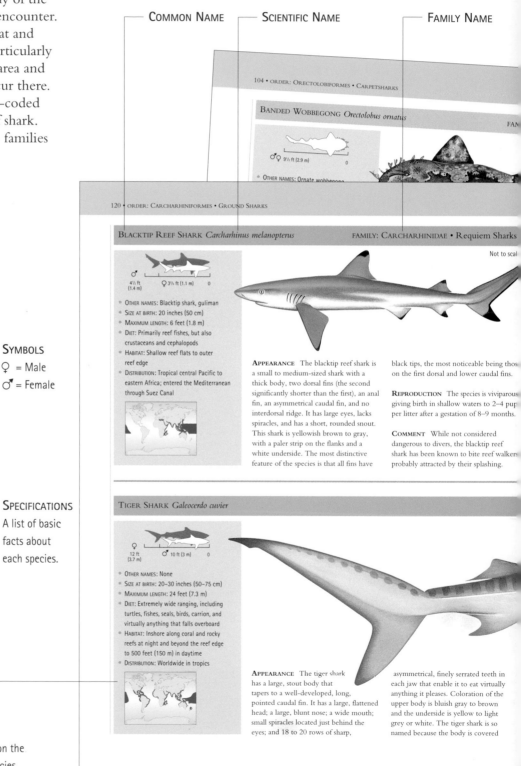

COMMON NAME   SCIENTIFIC NAME   FAMILY NAME

104 • ORDER: ORECTOLOBIFORMES • CARPETSHARKS

BANDED WOBBEGONG *Orectolobus ornatus*   FAM

♀♂ 9½ ft (2.9 m)   0

• OTHER NAMES: Ornate wobbegong

120 • ORDER: CARCHARHINIFORMES • GROUND SHARKS

BLACKTIP REEF SHARK *Carcharhinus melanopterus*   FAMILY: CARCHARHINIDAE • Requiem Sharks

Not to scal

♂ 4½ ft (1.4 m)   ♀ 3½ ft (1.1 m)   0

• OTHER NAMES: Blacktip shark, guliman
• SIZE AT BIRTH: 20 inches (50 cm)
• MAXIMUM LENGTH: 6 feet (1.8 m)
• DIET: Primarily reef fishes, but also crustaceans and cephalopods
• HABITAT: Shallow reef flats to outer reef edge
• DISTRIBUTION: Tropical central Pacific to eastern Africa; entered the Mediterranean through Suez Canal

APPEARANCE The blacktip reef shark is a small to medium-sized shark with a thick body, two dorsal fins (the second significantly shorter than the first), an anal fin, an asymmetrical caudal fin, and no interdorsal ridge. It has large eyes, lacks spiracles, and has a short, rounded snout. This shark is yellowish brown to gray, with a paler strip on the flanks and a white underside. The most distinctive feature of the species is that all fins have

black tips, the most noticeable being thos on the first dorsal and lower caudal fins.

REPRODUCTION The species is viviparous giving birth in shallow waters to 2–4 pup per litter after a gestation of 8–9 months.

COMMENT While not considered dangerous to divers, the blacktip reef shark has been known to bite reef walker probably attracted by their splashing.

TIGER SHARK *Galeocerdo cuvier*

♀ 12 ft (3.7 m)   ♂ 10 ft (3 m)   0

• OTHER NAMES: None
• SIZE AT BIRTH: 20–30 inches (50–75 cm)
• MAXIMUM LENGTH: 24 feet (7.3 m)
• DIET: Extremely wide ranging, including turtles, fishes, seals, birds, carrion, and virtually anything that falls overboard
• HABITAT: Inshore along coral and rocky reefs at night and beyond the reef edge to 500 feet (150 m) in daytime
• DISTRIBUTION: Worldwide in tropics

APPEARANCE The tiger shark has a large, stout body that tapers to a well-developed, long, pointed caudal fin. It has a large, flattened head; a large, blunt nose; a wide mouth; small spiracles located just behind the eyes; and 18 to 20 rows of sharp,

asymmetrical, finely serrated teeth in each jaw that enable it to eat virtually anything it pleases. Coloration of the upper body is bluish gray to brown and the underside is yellow to light grey or white. The tiger shark is so named because the body is covered

SIZE REFERENCE

Sharks vary tremendously in size, so the main illustrations are not drawn to scale. To indicate a species size, average measurements are provided. Where there is a significant size variation between sexes, outlines of males and females—which are white and gray respectively—have been included.

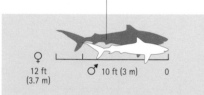

♀ 12 ft (3.7 m)   ♂ 10 ft (3 m)   0

SYMBOLS
♀ = Male
♂ = Female

• OTHER NAMES: None
• SIZE AT BIRTH: 20–30 inches (50–75 cm)
• MAXIMUM LENGTH: 24 feet (7.3 m)
• DIET: Extremely wide ranging, including turtles, fishes, seals, birds, carrion, and virtually anything that falls overboard
• HABITAT: Inshore along coral and rocky reefs at night and beyond the reef edge to 500 feet (150 m) in daytime
• DISTRIBUTION: Worldwide in tropics

SPECIFICATIONS
A list of basic facts about each species.

DISTRIBUTION MAP
Provides at-a-glance information on the worldwide distribution of each species.

APPEARANCE Provides a physical description of each species to help readers make accurate identifications from what may be only fleeting glimpses in the field.

REPRODUCTION Provides information on the method of reproduction used by the species and the size of its litters. For an explanation of the terms used here, see pages 78–81.

COMMENT Points of particular interest about the species are included here. Where a species poses a potential danger to swimmers or divers, this information is also provided.

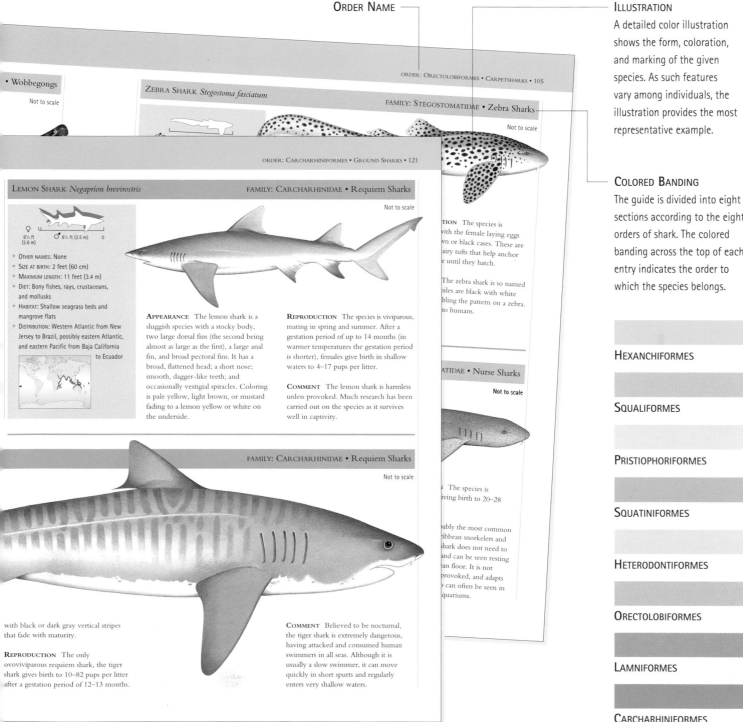

ORDER NAME

ILLUSTRATION
A detailed color illustration shows the form, coloration, and marking of the given species. As such features vary among individuals, the illustration provides the most representative example.

COLORED BANDING
The guide is divided into eight sections according to the eight orders of shark. The colored banding across the top of each entry indicates the order to which the species belongs.

HEXANCHIFORMES

SQUALIFORMES

PRISTIOPHORIFORMES

SQUATINIFORMES

HETERODONTIFORMES

ORECTOLOBIFORMES

LAMNIFORMES

CARCHARHINIFORMES

• Wobbegongs

Not to scale

ZEBRA SHARK *Stegostoma fasciatum*

FAMILY: STEGOSTOMATIDAE • Zebra Sharks

Not to scale

ORDER: ORECTOLOBIFORMES • CARPETSHARKS • 105

...TION The species is ...with the female laying eggs ...wn or black cases. These are ...airy tufts that help anchor ...e until they hatch.

...The zebra shark is so named ...niles are black with white ...bling the pattern on a zebra. ...to humans.

...ATIDAE • Nurse Sharks

Not to scale

...The species is ...iving birth to 20–28

...ably the most common ...ibbean snorkelers and ...shark does not need to ...and can be seen resting ...an floor. It is not ...provoked, and adapts ...o can often be seen in ...quariums.

ORDER: CARCHARHINIFORMES • GROUND SHARKS • 121

LEMON SHARK *Negaprion brevirostris*

FAMILY: CARCHARHINIDAE • Requiem Sharks

Not to scale

♀
8½ ft (2.6 m)   ♂ 8¼ ft (2.5 m)   0

- **OTHER NAMES:** None
- **SIZE AT BIRTH:** 2 feet (60 cm)
- **MAXIMUM LENGTH:** 11 feet (3.4 m)
- **DIET:** Bony fishes, rays, crustaceans, and mollusks
- **HABITAT:** Shallow seagrass beds and mangrove flats
- **DISTRIBUTION:** Western Atlantic from New Jersey to Brazil, possibly eastern Atlantic, and eastern Pacific from Baja California to Ecuador

APPEARANCE The lemon shark is a sluggish species with a stocky body, two large dorsal fins (the second being almost as large as the first), a large anal fin, and broad pectoral fins. It has a broad, flattened head; a short nose; smooth, dagger-like teeth; and occasionally vestigial spiracles. Coloring is pale yellow, light brown, or mustard fading to a lemon yellow or white on the underside.

REPRODUCTION The species is viviparous, mating in spring and summer. After a gestation period of up to 14 months (in warmer temperatures the gestation period is shorter), females give birth in shallow waters to 4–17 pups per litter.

COMMENT The lemon shark is harmless unless provoked. Much research has been carried out on the species as it survives well in captivity.

FAMILY: CARCHARHINIDAE • Requiem Sharks

Not to scale

with black or dark gray vertical stripes that fade with maturity.

REPRODUCTION The only ovoviviparous requiem shark, the tiger shark gives birth to 10–82 pups per litter after a gestation period of 12–13 months.

COMMENT Believed to be nocturnal, the tiger shark is extremely dangerous, having attacked and consumed human swimmers in all seas. Although it is usually a slow swimmer, it can move quickly in short spurts and regularly enters very shallow waters.

FRILLED SHARK *Chlamydoselachus anguineus*

FAMILY: CHLAMYDOSELACHIDAE • Frilled Sharks

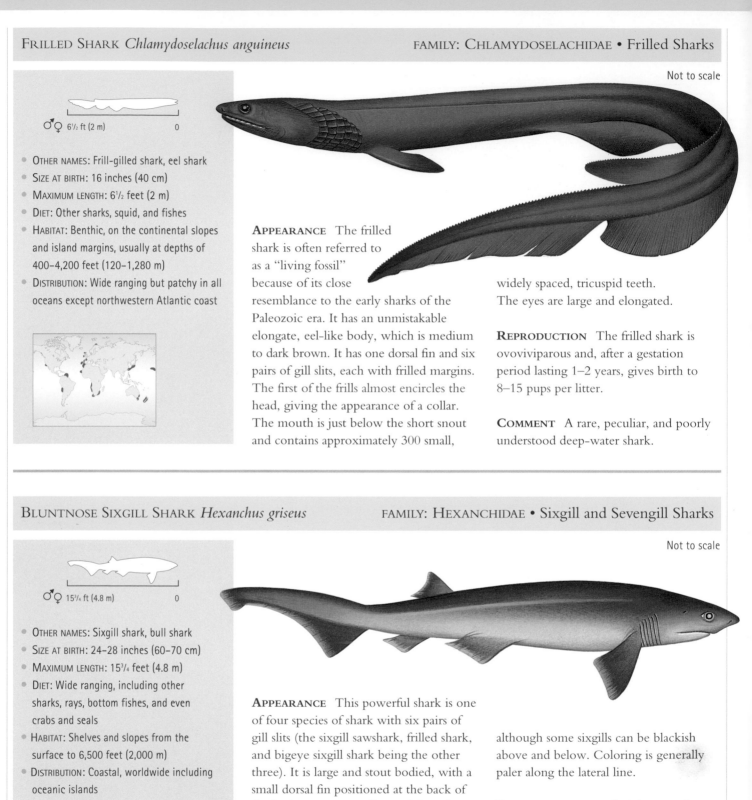

Not to scale

♂♀ 6½ ft (2 m) 0

- OTHER NAMES: Frill-gilled shark, eel shark
- SIZE AT BIRTH: 16 inches (40 cm)
- MAXIMUM LENGTH: 6½ feet (2 m)
- DIET: Other sharks, squid, and fishes
- HABITAT: Benthic, on the continental slopes and island margins, usually at depths of 400–4,200 feet (120–1,280 m)
- DISTRIBUTION: Wide ranging but patchy in all oceans except northwestern Atlantic coast

APPEARANCE The frilled shark is often referred to as a "living fossil" because of its close resemblance to the early sharks of the Paleozoic era. It has an unmistakable elongate, eel-like body, which is medium to dark brown. It has one dorsal fin and six pairs of gill slits, each with frilled margins. The first of the frills almost encircles the head, giving the appearance of a collar. The mouth is just below the short snout and contains approximately 300 small, widely spaced, tricuspid teeth. The eyes are large and elongated.

REPRODUCTION The frilled shark is ovoviviparous and, after a gestation period lasting 1–2 years, gives birth to 8–15 pups per litter.

COMMENT A rare, peculiar, and poorly understood deep-water shark.

BLUNTNOSE SIXGILL SHARK *Hexanchus griseus*

FAMILY: HEXANCHIDAE • Sixgill and Sevengill Sharks

Not to scale

♂♀ 15¾ ft (4.8 m) 0

- OTHER NAMES: Sixgill shark, bull shark
- SIZE AT BIRTH: 24–28 inches (60–70 cm)
- MAXIMUM LENGTH: 15¾ feet (4.8 m)
- DIET: Wide ranging, including other sharks, rays, bottom fishes, and even crabs and seals
- HABITAT: Shelves and slopes from the surface to 6,500 feet (2,000 m)
- DISTRIBUTION: Coastal, worldwide including oceanic islands

APPEARANCE This powerful shark is one of four species of shark with six pairs of gill slits (the sixgill sawshark, frilled shark, and bigeye sixgill shark being the other three). It is large and stout bodied, with a small dorsal fin positioned at the back of the body, an even smaller anal fin, a long tail, a broad head, and a broadly rounded snout. It has rows of large, comb-like teeth and the small, fluorescent-green eyes are set wide. Coloring is usually pale to dark gray or chocolate brown on the upper body and the underside is grayish white, although some sixgills can be blackish above and below. Coloring is generally paler along the lateral line.

REPRODUCTION Little is known about this species except that it is ovoviviparous, producing 22–108 pups per litter.

COMMENT This species is not considered dangerous to humans, although it may attack if provoked.

BROADNOSE SEVENGILL SHARK *Notorynchus cepedianus*   FAMILY: HEXANCHIDAE • Sixgill and Sevengill Sharks

Not to scale

♀ 8 ft (2.4 m)   ♂ 6¼ ft (1.9 m)   0

- OTHER NAMES: Cowshark, groundshark
- SIZE AT BIRTH: 16–18 inches (40–45 cm)
- MAXIMUM LENGTH: 10 feet (3 m)
- DIET: Wide ranging, including other sharks, rays, bottom fishes, and seals
- HABITAT: Shallow bays and estuaries along the continental shelf to 450 feet (135 m)
- DISTRIBUTION: Temperate coastal shelves, except for northern Atlantic

APPEARANCE One of only two species of shark with seven pairs of gills (the other being the sharpnose sevengill shark) the broadnose sevengill shark has a large, tapering body with one small dorsal fin. It has a broad head, blunt snout, and small eyes. The teeth are sharp and comb-like. The upper body is silvery gray to brown and speckled with distinctive dark gray or black spots. The underside is pale.

REPRODUCTION The broadnose sevengill shark is ovoviviparous, bearing up to 82 pups per litter. Females breed in spring and summer, and give birth in shallow bays.

COMMENT The species is still quite common off South Africa and Namibia. It has not been known to attack humans, but may be dangerous to incautious handlers.

BRAMBLE SHARK *Echinorhinus brucus*   FAMILY: ECHINORHINIDAE • Bramble Sharks

Not to scale

♀ 7¼ ft (2.2 m)   ♂ 5¼ ft (1.6 m)   0

- OTHER NAMES: Spinous shark
- SIZE AT BIRTH: 1–3 feet (30–90 cm)
- MAXIMUM LENGTH: 10 feet (3 m)
- DIET: Smaller sharks, bony fishes, and crabs
- HABITAT: Continental shelves and upper slopes, from 1,300–3,000 feet (400–900 m)
- DISTRIBUTION: Western Atlantic from Massachusetts to Virginia; Argentina; eastern Atlantic from North Sea to Mediterranean and southern Africa; India; New Zealand; southern Australia; and Japan

APPEARANCE This sluggish, deep-water shark has a stout body with two dorsal fins, a thick caudal fin, and no anal fin. The dorsal fins are of similar size, and are located at the back of the body, close to the pelvic and caudal fins. The eyes are relatively large, the snout is short, and the spiracles are small. The skin is a dark purplish gray to brown, often with darker spots on the back and sides, and there are large, spiny denticles that are irregularly scattered over the body.

REPRODUCTION The species is ovoviviparous, bearing 15–26 pups in each litter.

COMMENT Although sluggish, the bramble shark is capable of surprising speed in short bursts.

SPINY DOGFISH *Squalus acanthias*

Not to scale

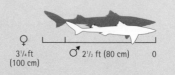

♀ 3¼ ft (100 cm)   ♂ 2½ ft (80 cm)   0

- OTHER NAMES: Piked dogfish, skittledog, white-spotted dogfish, spotted spiny dogfish, spurdog, Victorian spotted dogfish, codshark, thornshark
- SIZE AT BIRTH: 8–12 inches (20–30 cm)
- MAXIMUM LENGTH: 5 feet (1.5 m)
- DIET: Small fishes, krill, and squid
- HABITAT: Coastal, from very shallow water to 2,600 feet (800 m)
- DISTRIBUTION: Atlantic and Pacific oceans; southwest Australia; and tip of Africa

APPEARANCE The most common species of shark in the world, the slender spiny dogfish has two dorsal fins, the spines of which are mildly poisonous, and no anal fin. It has a long, pointed snout; large spiracles; and sharp, blade-like teeth. Coloring is bluish to gray, with a paler underside. The upper body and flanks are often covered with white spots that fade with age. The pectoral, pelvic, and caudal fins have pale posterior margins.

REPRODUCTION The species is ovoviviparous. After a gestation period of 18–24 months, females give birth to 1–20 pups per litter in large bays and estuaries.

COMMENT While still probably the world's most abundant shark, this long-lived (to 70 years), bottom-dwelling species is severely depleted due to overfishing.

SMALLFIN GULPER SHARK *Centrophorus moluccensis*

Not to scale

♀ 39 in (98 cm)   ♂ 34 in (86 cm)   0

- OTHER NAMES: Endeavour dogfish, arrowspine dogfish
- SIZE AT BIRTH: 12–15 inches (30–38 cm)
- MAXIMUM LENGTH: 39 inches (98 cm)
- DIET: Pelagic and bottom fishes, small dogfish sharks, squid, octopus, shrimp, and tunicates
- HABITAT: Benthic, on the outer continental shelves and upper slopes at depths of 420–2,700 feet (130–820 m)
- DISTRIBUTION: Indo-West Pacific; scattered records from eastern coast of South Africa eastward to Australia and Japan

APPEARANCE This slender, elegant deep-water shark has two dorsal fins with grooved spines (the second fin is small); elongated, pectoral fins with pointed rear tips; and no anal fin. It has blade-like teeth in both jaws; a long, narrow snout; large, green eyes; and is covered in smooth, flat denticles. Coloring is light gray to gray-brown on the upper body and fins, and white on the underside. It has dusky or black blotches on the tips of the dorsal fins and upper lobe of the caudal fin.

REPRODUCTION The smallfin gulper shark is ovoviviparous, giving birth in summer to two pups per litter. It has a gestation period of at least one year but possibly as long as two years.

COMMENT A common deep-water shark in some areas, numbers of smallfin gulper sharks have decreased significantly due to overfishing. The young often have a pair of barbs on the dorsal fin spines, which resemble an arrowhead.

BLACKBELLY LANTERNSHARK *Etmopterus lucifer*

FAMILY ETMOPTERIDAE • Lanternsharks

Not to scale

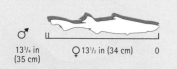

♂
13³/₄ in
(35 cm)   ♀ 13½ in (34 cm)   0

- OTHER NAMES: Lucifer shark
- SIZE AT BIRTH: 6 inches (15 cm)
- MAXIMUM LENGTH: 18 inches (45 cm)
- DIET: Squid, shrimp, and small fishes
- HABITAT: Along slopes and shelves at depths of 590–3,300 feet (180–1,000 m)
- DISTRIBUTION: Southern and eastern Australia; New Zealand; and China Sea to Japan (Records from southern Africa and South America possibly not this species)

APPEARANCE A small and slender shark, the blackbelly lanternshark has two spined dorsal fins (the second being about twice the size of the first) and no anal fin. It has large eyes, spiracles, and nostrils; a short snout; and blade-like teeth. The upper body is light brown changing to a darker brown on the flanks to nearly black on the lower body, with black markings on the underside.

REPRODUCTION It is presumed this species is ovoviviparous, but little is known of its reproductive biology or the size of the litter.

COMMENT The lanternshark is so called because of the bioluminescent organs that run along its underside. These enable it to blend in with the weak illumination from the surface, providing camouflage.

GREENLAND SLEEPER SHARK *Somniosus microcephalus*

FAMILY: SOMNIOSIDAE • Sleeper Sharks

Not to scale

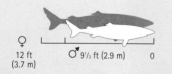

♀
12 ft
(3.7 m)   ♂ 9½ ft (2.9 m)   0

- OTHER NAMES: Sleeper shark, gurry shark
- SIZE AT BIRTH: 15 inches (38 cm)
- MAXIMUM LENGTH: 21 feet (6.4 m)
- DIET: Seals, bottom fishes, invertebrates, and carrion
- HABITAT: From shallow water to 1,800 feet (550 m)
- DISTRIBUTION: North Atlantic Ocean

APPEARANCE The Greenland sleeper shark is a gigantic, nearly cylindrical shark with two small dorsal fins, an asymmetrical caudal fin, and no anal fin. It has a short, rounded snout; green eyes; relatively large spiracles; and long, pointed teeth. It is grayish pink in color, with darker, bluish black fins. Although sluggish, the species can catch fast-moving prey, which are possibly attracted to the shark by the bioluminescent parasitic copepods that attach themselves to the corneas of the shark's eyes.

REPRODUCTION The species is ovoviviparous, bearing approximately 10 pups per litter.

COMMENT The Greenland sleeper shark is the only Atlantic polar shark living in water temperatures of 36°F to 45°F (2°C to 7°C). It does not attack humans.

PRICKLY DOGFISH *Oxynotus bruniensis*

Not to scale

♀ 2²/₅ ft (73 cm)   ♂ 2 ft (60 cm)   0

- OTHER NAMES: None
- SIZE AT BIRTH: 4 inches (10 cm)
- MAXIMUM LENGTH: 2²/₅ feet (73 cm)
- DIET: Bottom invertebrates
- HABITAT: Temperate waters, from 165–1,640 feet (50–500 m)
- DISTRIBUTION: Southern Australia and New Zealand

APPEARANCE
An unusual-looking and harmless shark, the prickly dogfish has a stout body that is laterally triangular in shape. It has two large, high, spined dorsal fins; small gill slits; a visible ridge on the abdomen; and no anal fin. It has a somewhat flattened head with prominent spiracles, large eyes, a short snout, and a small, slot-like mouth. The skin is covered in small, prickly denticles, making it extremely rough. It is either dull gray or brown with whitish to translucent margins on the dorsal, pectoral, and pelvic fins.

REPRODUCTION
The prickly dogfish is ovoviviparous, giving birth to approximately seven pups per litter.

COMMENT
One of only four species of roughshark, very little is known about this curious benthic shark.

COOKIECUTTER SHARK *Isistius brasiliensis*

Not to scale

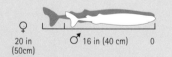

♀ 20 in (50cm)   ♂ 16 in (40 cm)   0

- OTHER NAMES: Cigar shark, luminous shark
- SIZE AT BIRTH: Unknown
- MAXIMUM LENGTH: 20 inches (50 cm)
- DIET: Squid, and pieces of large fishes and marine mammals
- HABITAT: Oceanic, migrating from depths of 3,300 feet (1,000 m) to the surface each night
- DISTRIBUTION: Widespread, mostly oceanic

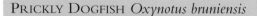

APPEARANCE
This chocolate-colored, cigar-shaped shark has two small dorsal fins located to the rear of the body, a nearly symmetrical caudal fin, and no anal fin. It has a dark band around the gill slits; large eyes with green pupils; a short, conical snout; and fleshy, suctorial lips. The enlarged, sharp, triangular teeth enable the cookiecutter shark to take bites of flesh from its prey, leaving a distinctive circular scar.

REPRODUCTION
The cookiecutter shark is ovoviviparous, but little is known about its reproductive biology or the size of the litter.

COMMENT
The species has the ability to turn a luminous green, possibly as a means of attracting prey. It attacks and removes plugs of flesh from large tunas, billfishes, seals, and whales, and has even attacked a nuclear submarine.

SPINED PYGMY SHARK *Squaliolus laticaudus*

Not to scale

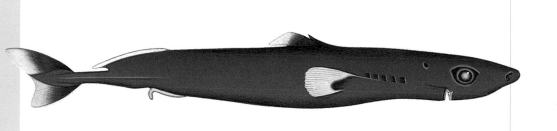

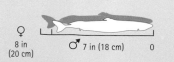

♀ 8 in (20 cm) ♂ 7 in (18 cm) 0

- OTHER NAMES: Dwarf shark, midwater shark
- SIZE AT BIRTH: Less than ½ inch (12 mm)
- MAXIMUM LENGTH: 10 inches (25 cm)
- DIET: Squid, shrimp, and midwater fishes
- HABITAT: Offshore, at depths of 650–6,500 feet (200–2,000 m)
- DISTRIBUTION: All oceans

APPEARANCE The spined pygmy shark has a spindle-shaped body; two dorsal fins; small, rounded pectoral fins; an almost symmetrical caudal fin; and no anal fin. The first dorsal fin is significantly smaller than the second, and is the only one to have a spine. It has large eyes, large spiracles, and a pointed snout. It is dark brown to jet black with lighter fin margins. Its ventral surface is bioluminescent, which may help the shark blend in with weak illumination from the surface when viewed from below.

REPRODUCTION This species is probably ovoviviparous but little is known of its reproductive biology or litter size.

COMMENT This harmless shark is one of the smallest species in the world.

COMMON SAWSHARK *Pristiophorus cirratus*

Not to scale

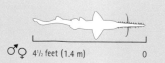

♂♀ 4½ feet (1.4 m) 0

- OTHER NAMES: Longnose sawshark
- SIZE AT BIRTH: 11–15 inches (27–38 cm)
- MAXIMUM LENGTH: 4½ feet (1.4 m)
- DIET: Small bony fishes
- HABITAT: Continental shelves and slopes to about 1,000 feet (300 m)
- DISTRIBUTION: Southern Australia

APPEARANCE This medium-sized shark has a slender, elongate body with large pectoral fins, two dorsal fins, and no anal fin. The head is depressed and the long, flattened snout (comprising up to 30 percent of the shark's length) resembles a saw, with teeth on the edges and two barbels midway. The shark is sandy to grayish brown with irregular brown splotches. The underside is pale and the snout is pinkish. The skin is covered in tiny denticles giving it a soft feel, and the dorsal and pectoral fins are scaly.

REPRODUCTION The species is ovoviviparous, breeding in winter, with 3–22 pups per litter. The pups are born with the teeth of the saw folded back against the blade, to avoid injuring the mother during birth.

COMMENT The harmless sawshark, one of five species in the family, is sometimes confused with sawfishes, which are elongate rays.

PACIFIC ANGELSHARK *Squatina californica*

FAMILY: SQUATINIDAE • Angelsharks

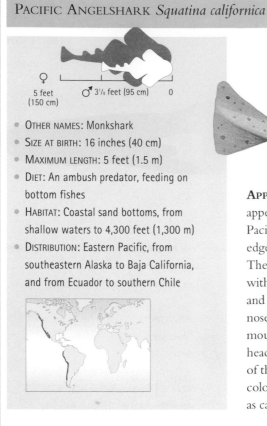

Not to scale

♀ 5 feet (150 cm) ♂ 3⅛ feet (95 cm) 0

- OTHER NAMES: Monkshark
- SIZE AT BIRTH: 16 inches (40 cm)
- MAXIMUM LENGTH: 5 feet (1.5 m)
- DIET: An ambush predator, feeding on bottom fishes
- HABITAT: Coastal sand bottoms, from shallow waters to 4,300 feet (1,300 m)
- DISTRIBUTION: Eastern Pacific, from southeastern Alaska to Baja California, and from Ecuador to southern Chile

APPEARANCE Ray-like in appearance, the largely nocturnal Pacific angelshark is flattened, with the edges of the pectorals free from the body. The pectoral and pelvic fins are broad with rounded tips and the dorsal, anal, and caudal fins are small. It has a blunt nose, large spiracles, and a terminal mouth. The eyes are located on top of the head and the gill slits are on the underside of the body. It is a rather sluggish shark, colored speckled sandy to gray or brown as camouflage. The underside is white.

REPRODUCTION Ovoviviparous, giving birth to about 8–13 pups per litter; the larger the female, the larger the litter.

COMMENT The species is not considered dangerous but will bite if surprised or provoked. Numbers are declining as a result of overfishing.

CALIFORNIAN HORNSHARK *Heterodontus francisci*

FAMILY: HETERODONTIDAE • Hornsharks

Not to scale

♂ 25 in (64 cm) ♀ 23 in (58 cm) 0

- OTHER NAMES: Bullhead shark, hornshark
- SIZE AT BIRTH: 6 inches (15 cm)
- MAXIMUM LENGTH: 4 feet (1.2 m), but rarely larger than 3 feet (1 m)
- DIET: Sea urchins, crustaceans, and small fishes
- HABITAT: Among large rocks at the base of kelp beds
- DISTRIBUTION: Central California to Baja California

APPEARANCE The Californian hornshark is an unusual-looking, sluggish, medium-sized shark with two spined dorsal fins and an anal fin. It uses its large, specialized pectoral fins to "walk" along the ocean floor. It has an enlarged head with prominent ridges over the large eyes, and a pig-like snout. The skin is sandy to gray, usually with dark spots, and yellow on the underside. It is rough in texture.

REPRODUCTION The species is oviparous, laying two eggs a month for three months of the year. The mother carries the brown, corkscrew-shaped egg cases in her mouth, before wedging them into crevices for protection. They hatch after 7–9 months.

COMMENT Popular in public aquariums, this sedentary species defies the mistaken belief that all sharks must swim in order to breathe.

NECKLACE CARPETSHARK *Parascyllium variolatum*

FAMILY: PARASCYLLIIDAE • Collared Carpetsharks

Not to scale

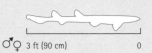

♂♀ 3 ft (90 cm)　　　　0

- OTHER NAMES: Varied carpetshark, southern carpetshark, varied catshark
- SIZE AT BIRTH: Unknown
- MAXIMUM LENGTH: 3 feet (90 cm)
- DIET: Unknown, however the dentition would suggest benthic crustaceans
- HABITAT: Continental shelves to 1,600 feet (500 m)
- DISTRIBUTION: Southwestern Australia to southern Australia

APPEARANCE

Somewhat eel-like in appearance, the necklace carpetshark has an elongate, slender, and tubular body. It has two dorsal fins of similar size, an anal fin, and a long caudal fin. The head and snout are slightly depressed, the eyes are oval and set well behind the mouth, the spiracles are small, and two short barbels hang from the underside of the snout. It is fawn with brown and white spots all over the body. A wide, dark collar speckled with white spots encircles the neck around the gills, and there are black saddles near the fin margins.

REPRODUCTION
This species is oviparous, but little else is known about its reproductive biology.

COMMENT
Very little is known about this harmless and extraordinarily beautiful species of shark.

BLIND SHARK *Brachaelurus waddi*

FAMILY: BRACHAELURIDAE • Blind Sharks

Not to scale

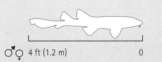

♂♀ 4 ft (1.2 m)　　　　0

- OTHER NAMES: Brown catshark
- SIZE AT BIRTH: 7 inches (18 cm)
- MAXIMUM LENGTH: 4 feet (1.2 m)
- DIET: Reef fish and invertebrates
- HABITAT: Rocky shores from tidepools to 330 feet (100 m)
- DISTRIBUTION: Central eastern Australia

APPEARANCE
A nocturnal shark, the blind shark has a stout body with two close-set dorsal fins of similar size, an anal fin, and a long caudal fin. It has a depressed head, large spiracles below the small eyes, well-developed nostrils, and long nasal barbels. The smooth skin is covered in small denticles. Coloring is light to blackish brown with a yellowish brown underside. The body and fins are usually speckled with numerous small white spots. The young have prominent, broad, dusky cross-bands that disappear as the shark ages.

REPRODUCTION
The blind shark is ovoviviparous, giving birth to 7–8 pups per litter in late spring or summer.

COMMENT
This harmless species is not blind, but appears to be so as it rotates its eyeballs backward when frightened, such as when taken from the water.

BANDED WOBBEGONG *Orectolobus ornatus*

FAMILY: ORECTOLOBIDAE • Wobbegongs

Not to scale

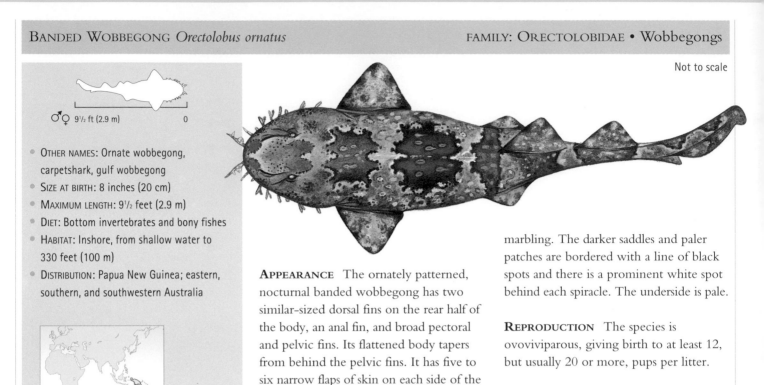

♂♀ 9½ ft (2.9 m)   0

- OTHER NAMES: Ornate wobbegong, carpetshark, gulf wobbegong
- SIZE AT BIRTH: 8 inches (20 cm)
- MAXIMUM LENGTH: 9½ feet (2.9 m)
- DIET: Bottom invertebrates and bony fishes
- HABITAT: Inshore, from shallow water to 330 feet (100 m)
- DISTRIBUTION: Papua New Guinea; eastern, southern, and southwestern Australia

APPEARANCE The ornately patterned, nocturnal banded wobbegong has two similar-sized dorsal fins on the rear half of the body, an anal fin, and broad pectoral and pelvic fins. Its flattened body tapers from behind the pelvic fins. It has five to six narrow flaps of skin on each side of the head, two nasal barbels, sharp teeth, and large spiracles. Well camouflaged, the species is brown with light and dark marbling. The darker saddles and paler patches are bordered with a line of black spots and there is a prominent white spot behind each spiracle. The underside is pale.

REPRODUCTION The species is ovoviviparous, giving birth to at least 12, but usually 20 or more, pups per litter.

COMMENT Harmless to humans, this and five other species of wobbegong are common, but often overlooked by divers.

EPAULETTE SHARK *Hemiscyllium ocellatum*

FAMILY: HEMISCYLLIIDAE • Longtailed Carpetsharks

Not to scale

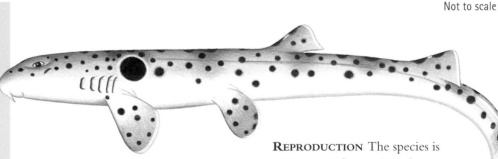

♂♀ 3½ ft (107 cm)   0

- OTHER NAMES: Ocellated bambooshark
- SIZE AT BIRTH: 6 inches (15 cm)
- MAXIMUM LENGTH: 3½ feet (107 cm)
- DIET: Benthic invertebrates
- HABITAT: Shallow inshore reefs
- DISTRIBUTION: New Guinea; northwest to northeastern Australia

APPEARANCE The epaulette shark has a slender body with two dorsal fins of similar size and an anal fin set well back. It has a rounded snout, two short nasal barbels, and large spiracles. The color pattern is designed for camouflage, and is either golden or tan with large, widely spaced black spots. It also has a distinctive large black ocellus with a white margin located behind each set of gills. The young are born with black bands, which transform to spots as they age.

REPRODUCTION The species is oviparous. After mating, the female lays two eggs at night in brown, ellipsoidal cases, which are about 4 inches (10 cm) long. The cases hatch in about 130 days.

COMMENT The epaulette shark is well suited to aquarium captivity, where females have been known to lay 50 fertile eggs per year.

ZEBRA SHARK *Stegostoma fasciatum*

FAMILY: STEGOSTOMATIDAE • Zebra Sharks

Not to scale

♂♀ 6½ ft (2 m)   0

- OTHER NAMES: Leopard shark, blind shark
- SIZE AT BIRTH: 8 inches (20 cm)
- MAXIMUM LENGTH: 11½ feet (3.5 m)
- DIET: Mollusks, crustaceans, and bony fishes
- HABITAT: Shallow water; common in coral reefs
- DISTRIBUTION: Tropical western Pacific to eastern Africa

APPEARANCE Easily recognizable by its elongate, blade-like tail, which is almost half its total length, the zebra shark has a stout body; two close-set dorsal fins; an anal fin; large, rounded pectoral fins; and prominent ridges that run along the upper body. It has a broad head, short snout, short nasal barbels, and large spiracles. Although it has five gill openings, the fourth and fifth overlap. Coloring of adults is yellowish to brown with dark spots, and the underside is pale.

REPRODUCTION The species is oviparous, with the female laying eggs in large brown or black cases. These are covered in hairy tufts that help anchor them in place until they hatch.

COMMENT The zebra shark is so named because juveniles are black with white stripes, resembling the pattern on a zebra. It is harmless to humans.

NURSE SHARK *Ginglymostoma cirratum*

FAMILY: GINGLYMOSTOMATIDAE • Nurse Sharks

Not to scale

♀ 8¼ ft (2.5 m)   ♂ 8 ft (2.4 m)   0

- OTHER NAMES: None
- SIZE AT BIRTH: 11–12 inches (27–30 cm)
- MAXIMUM LENGTH: 14 feet (4.3 m), but rarely larger than 10 feet (3 m)
- DIET: Primarily benthic crustaceans, shellfish, octopus, squid, and very slow fishes
- HABITAT: Shallow inshore reefs and mangrove flats to 40 feet (12 m)
- DISTRIBUTION: Western Atlantic from Rhode Island to Brazil; eastern Atlantic; and eastern Pacific from Mexico to Peru

APPEARANCE The nurse shark is a sluggish, nocturnal species with large, rounded dorsal and pectoral fins, an anal fin, and a relatively long caudal fin. The dorsal fins are set to the rear of the body. It has a small spiracle below each eye; small, sharp teeth; nasal grooves that run between the nostrils and the corner of the mouth; and nasal barbels. It is yellowish brown or tan to dark brown and lighter on the lower body. Juveniles have black spots that fade with age.

REPRODUCTION The species is ovoviviparous, giving birth to 20–28 pups per litter.

COMMENT Probably the most common shark seen by Caribbean snorkelers and divers, the nurse shark does not need to swim to breathe, and can be seen resting quietly on the ocean floor. It is not aggressive, unless provoked, and adapts well to captivity so can often be seen in oceanariums and aquariums.

WHALE SHARK *Rhincodon typus*

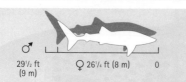

♂ 29½ ft (9 m) ♀ 26¼ ft (8 m) 0

- OTHER NAMES: None
- SIZE AT BIRTH: 18 inches (45 cm)
- MAXIMUM LENGTH: 46 feet (14 m)
- DIET: Filter feeds on plankton and small fishes
- HABITAT: Ocean and coastal zones, often entering lagoons
- DISTRIBUTION: Worldwide in tropics

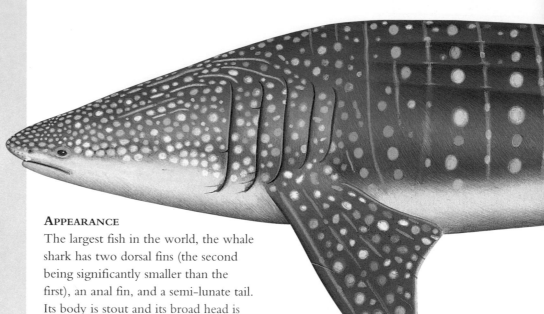

APPEARANCE

The largest fish in the world, the whale shark has two dorsal fins (the second being significantly smaller than the first), an anal fin, and a semi-lunate tail. Its body is stout and its broad head is depressed. Each jaw of this enormous filter feeder is lined with 300 rows of

GOBLIN SHARK *Mitsukurina owstoni*

FAMILY: MITSUKURINIDAE • Goblin Sharks

Not to scale

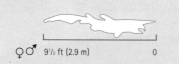

♀♂ 9½ ft (2.9 m) 0

- OTHER NAMES: Elfin shark
- SIZE AT BIRTH: Unknown
- MAXIMUM LENGTH: 12¾ feet (3.9 cm)
- DIET: Little is known. However, its fragile, pointed teeth indicate soft-bodied prey such as pelagic squid and shrimp
- HABITAT: Upper continental slope, near the bottom, at 1,180–1,800 feet (360–550 m)
- DISTRIBUTION: Scattered tropical and temperate locations in the Atlantic, Indian, and Pacific oceans

APPEARANCE A large shark with a flabby body, two dorsal fins of similar size, and an anal fin, the bottom-dwelling goblin shark is light pinkish gray, with the gill area and fins a slightly darker shade. Its most distinctive feature is the flat, elongate snout that extends far in front of the long mouth. The jaw protrudes prominently when extended. It has pointed teeth and tiny eyes.

REPRODUCTION It is presumed the species is ovoviviparous, but little is known about its biology or the size of its litter.

COMMENT Until the late 1890s when rediscovered, it was assumed the goblin shark had been extinct for 100 million years. There is still very little known about this bizarre-looking deep-water shark, the sole member of its family.

FAMILY: RHINCODONTIDAE • Whale Sharks

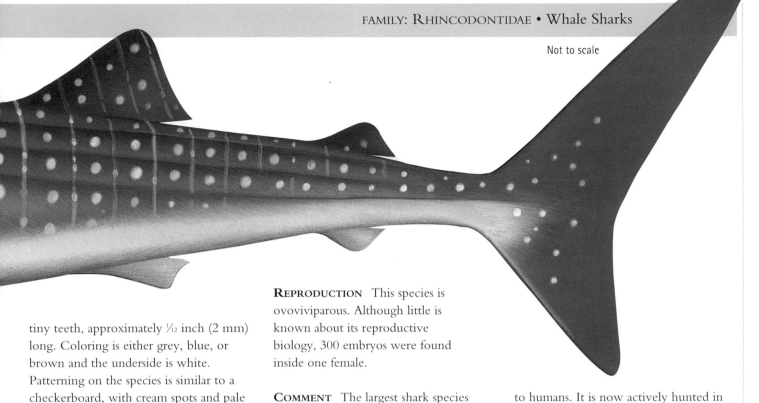

Not to scale

tiny teeth, approximately 1/12 inch (2 mm) long. Coloring is either grey, blue, or brown and the underside is white. Patterning on the species is similar to a checkerboard, with cream spots and pale vertical and horizontal lines.

REPRODUCTION This species is ovoviviparous. Although little is known about its reproductive biology, 300 embryos were found inside one female.

COMMENT The largest shark species in the world, the whale shark is harmless to humans. It is now actively hunted in the western Pacific Ocean.

SAND TIGER SHARK *Carcharias taurus*

FAMILY: ODONTASPIDIDAE • Sand Tiger Sharks

Not to scale

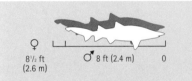

♀ 8½ ft (2.6 m)   ♂ 8 ft (2.4 m)   0

- OTHER NAMES: Raggedtooth shark, gray nurse shark, spotted raggedtooth shark, sand shark
- SIZE AT BIRTH: 3¼ feet (1 m)
- MAXIMUM LENGTH: 10½ feet (3.2 m)
- DIET: Fishes, sharks, rays, crabs, and lobsters
- HABITAT: Coastal, from sandy beaches and reefs to 625 feet (190 m)
- DISTRIBUTION: Northwestern and eastern Atlantic, Gulf of Mexico, Argentina, southern Africa, Red Sea, Australia, and China Sea to Sea of Japan, Indonesia, and possibly Oman, Pakistan, and India

APPEARANCE The sand tiger shark has a bulky, stout body. It has two large dorsal fins, which are roughly the same size as the anal fin, and an asymmetrical caudal fin with a long upper lobe. It has small, light-colored eyes, a pointed snout, a long mouth, and dagger-like teeth. The upper body is lightish brown or sandy, paler on the underside, and covered with small yellow spots that fade as the shark grows.

REPRODUCTION This species is viviparous and exhibits a form of uterine cannibalism called adelophagy (see page 80). During the 9–12 month gestation period, the strongest embryo in each of the two uterine chambers eats its siblings and is then nurtured on unfertilized eggs until birth.

COMMENT Despite its fearsome appearance, the sand tiger shark is not considered dangerous to humans.

CROCODILE SHARK *Pseudocarcharias kamoharai*

Not to scale

♀ 3⅛ ft (95 cm)   ♂ 3 ft (90 cm)   0

- OTHER NAMES: None
- SIZE AT BIRTH: 16 inches (40 cm)
- MAXIMUM LENGTH: 3¼ feet (1 m)
- DIET: Probably small fishes, squid, and crustaceans
- HABITAT: Oceanic, probably midwater, from the surface to 1,900 feet (590 m), and occasionally inshore
- DISTRIBUTION: All tropical and subtropical seas

APPEARANCE The crocodile shark has a relatively long, slender body with two dorsal fins (the first significantly larger than the second), an anal fin, rounded pectoral fins, and an asymmetrical caudal fin. It has a long, rounded snout; large eyes without nictitating membranes; long, dagger-like teeth; and long gill slits. The species is gray to dark brown on the upper body and paler on the underside. It has white fin margins.

REPRODUCTION The species is viviparous, giving birth to 4 pups per litter. As with the sand tiger shark, the crocodile shark has a form of uterine cannibalism called adelophagy (see page 80). However, unlike the sand tiger shark, two embryos survive from within each uterine chamber.

COMMENT Little is known about the crocodile shark although it is thought to be nocturnal.

THRESHER SHARK *Alopias vulpinus*

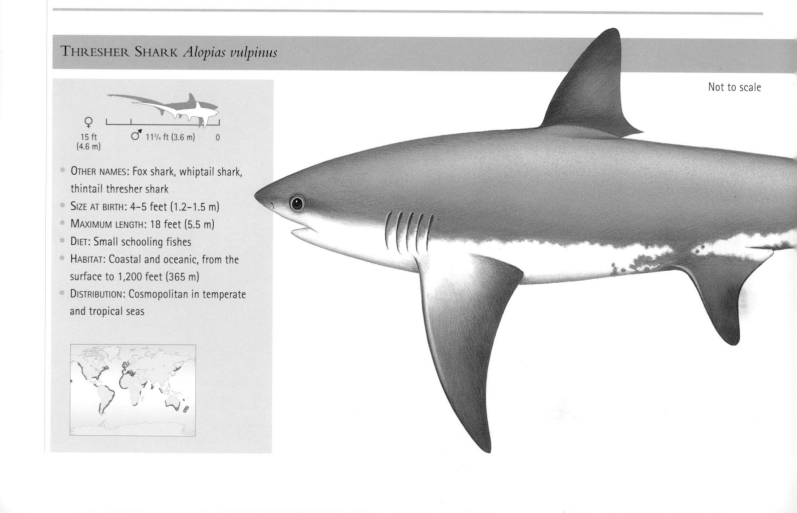

Not to scale

♀ 15 ft (4.6 m)   ♂ 11¾ ft (3.6 m)   0

- OTHER NAMES: Fox shark, whiptail shark, thintail thresher shark
- SIZE AT BIRTH: 4–5 feet (1.2–1.5 m)
- MAXIMUM LENGTH: 18 feet (5.5 m)
- DIET: Small schooling fishes
- HABITAT: Coastal and oceanic, from the surface to 1,200 feet (365 m)
- DISTRIBUTION: Cosmopolitan in temperate and tropical seas

MEGAMOUTH SHARK *Megachasma pelagios*

Not to scale

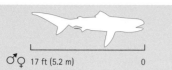

♂♀ 17 ft (5.2 m)   0

- OTHER NAMES: None
- SIZE AT BIRTH: Unknown
- MAXIMUM LENGTH: 17 feet (5.2 m)
- DIET: Filter feeds primarily on crustaceans
- HABITAT: Oceanic and coastal, probably at 500–3,300 feet (150–1,000 m), migrating toward the surface at night
- DISTRIBUTION: Found in all oceans

APPEARANCE Only recently discovered, the megamouth has a large, flabby body; two dorsal fins (the first significantly larger than the second); an anal fin; long, narrow pectoral fins; and an asymmetrical caudal fin with a long upper lobe. As its common name suggests, it has an enormous mouth, extending behind the eyes and measuring over 40 inches (1 m) in width, with over 100 rows of tiny teeth. The mouth is luminous, enabling it to attract plankton. Coloring is dark brown or gray to black, lighter on the flanks to pale on the underside, and there are white margins on the fins.

REPRODUCTION Nothing is known of the reproductive biology or litter numbers of this species.

COMMENT The sole member of its family, the megamouth shark was discovered off Hawaii in 1976.

FAMILY: ALOPIIDAE • Thresher Sharks

APPEARANCE The thresher shark has a large, stout body with large pelvic fins, two dorsal fins (the second of which is minute), a tiny anal fin, and broad pectoral fins with pointed tips. It has a short snout; large eyes without nictitating membranes; a small mouth filled with rows of small, sharp teeth; and fairly short gill slits. The most distinctive feature of the thresher shark is the long upper lobe of the caudal fin, which is equal in length to the rest of the body. Coloring is pale to dark gray, paler on the underside.

REPRODUCTION The species is ovo-viviparous and oophagous (see page 80), giving birth to 2–4 pups per litter after a gestation period estimated at 9 months.

COMMENT The thresher shark uses its elongate tail to herd its prey into groups and stun them. It is harmless to humans but people should be cautious and remain a safe distance from its tail. Numbers have significantly decreased due to overfishing.

BASKING SHARK *Cetorhinus maximus*

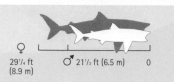

♀ 29¼ ft (8.9 m)   ♂ 21⅓ ft (6.5 m)   0

- OTHER NAMES: Bone shark, elephant shark, sailfish shark
- SIZE AT BIRTH: 5–6½ feet (1.5–2.0 m) (est.)
- MAXIMUM LENGTH: 49¼ feet (15 m), but few exceed 33 feet (10 m)
- DIET: Filter feeds on plankton and small crustaceans
- HABITAT: Coastal, usually seen near the surface
- DISTRIBUTION: Most temperate seas, but not in

Indian Ocean except south-western Australia and southeastern South Africa

APPEARANCE The basking shark is an extremely large species with a stocky body, two dorsal fins (the second significantly smaller than the first), an anal fin, and a lunate caudal fin. It has large gill rakers, very long and broad gill slits, a conical pointed snout, and minute teeth. Coloring is dark blue, brown, charcoal, or gray, paler on the underside.

GREAT WHITE SHARK   *Carcharodon carcharias*

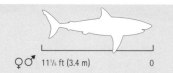

♀♂ 11⅙ ft (3.4 m)   0

- OTHER NAMES: White shark, white death, white pointer, blue pointer
- SIZE AT BIRTH: 3–4 feet (90–120 cm)
- MAXIMUM LENGTH: Reports of 24 feet (7.3 m)
- DIET: Seals, sea lions, dolphins, porpoises, other sharks, carrion, seabirds, turtles, large bony fishes, and invertebrates
- HABITAT: Coastal cooler waters with seal colonies from the surface to 4,200 feet (1,280 m), extending to tropics and open ocean

- DISTRIBUTION: Worldwide in temperate seas, also Hawaii (rarely)

APPEARANCE The great white shark has a stout body with two dorsal fins; long, narrow pectoral fins; a lunate caudal fin; and an anal fin. The second dorsal and anal fins are small. It has large gill slits; a short, conical snout; black eyes; and serrated, triangular, razor-sharp teeth. The upper body is either slate brown,

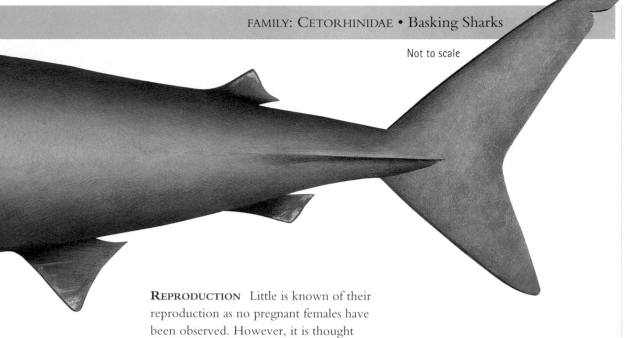

FAMILY: CETORHINIDAE • Basking Sharks

Not to scale

REPRODUCTION Little is known of their reproduction as no pregnant females have been observed. However, it is thought that they are ovoviviparous and oophagous (see page 80). Litter size is unknown.

COMMENT This is the second largest species of shark, and is occasionally killed for its oil (squalene), fins, skin, and meat. It is thought that it loses its gill rakers during winter when food is scarce, and is unable to eat until they grow back 4–5 months later.

FAMILY: LAMNIDAE • Mackerel Sharks

Not to scale

charcoal, or blue gray while the lower body is white or cream.

REPRODUCTION The species is viviparous and oophagous (see page 80). The female gives birth to 7–9 offspring per litter.

COMMENT The largest of the flesh-eating sharks, the great white is considered to be the most dangerous temperate shark to humans. As fishing is seriously depleting numbers, the species is now protected in California, South Africa, Maldives, Namibia, Israel, and much of Australia.

SHORTFIN MAKO *Isurus oxyrinchus*

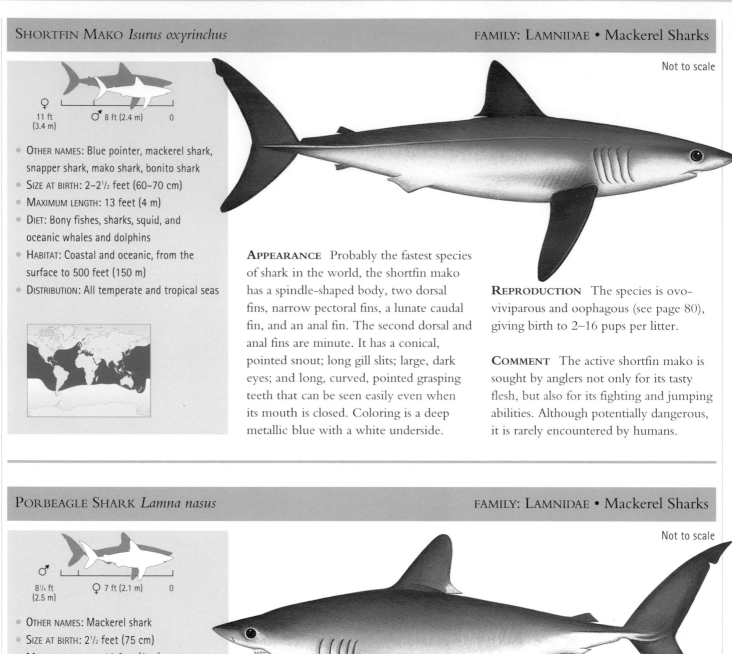

Not to scale

♀ 11 ft (3.4 m)   ♂ 8 ft (2.4 m)   0

- OTHER NAMES: Blue pointer, mackerel shark, snapper shark, mako shark, bonito shark
- SIZE AT BIRTH: 2–2½ feet (60–70 cm)
- MAXIMUM LENGTH: 13 feet (4 m)
- DIET: Bony fishes, sharks, squid, and oceanic whales and dolphins
- HABITAT: Coastal and oceanic, from the surface to 500 feet (150 m)
- DISTRIBUTION: All temperate and tropical seas

APPEARANCE Probably the fastest species of shark in the world, the shortfin mako has a spindle-shaped body, two dorsal fins, narrow pectoral fins, a lunate caudal fin, and an anal fin. The second dorsal and anal fins are minute. It has a conical, pointed snout; long gill slits; large, dark eyes; and long, curved, pointed grasping teeth that can be seen easily even when its mouth is closed. Coloring is a deep metallic blue with a white underside.

REPRODUCTION The species is ovoviviparous and oophagous (see page 80), giving birth to 2–16 pups per litter.

COMMENT The active shortfin mako is sought by anglers not only for its tasty flesh, but also for its fighting and jumping abilities. Although potentially dangerous, it is rarely encountered by humans.

PORBEAGLE SHARK *Lamna nasus*

Not to scale

♂ 8¼ ft (2.5 m)   ♀ 7 ft (2.1 m)   0

- OTHER NAMES: Mackerel shark
- SIZE AT BIRTH: 2½ feet (75 cm)
- MAXIMUM LENGTH: 10 feet (3 m)
- DIET: Bony fishes, other sharks, and squid
- HABITAT: Inshore and oceanic from the surface to 1,200 feet (370 m)
- DISTRIBUTION: Most temperate seas except North Pacific

APPEARANCE
The porbeagle is an extremely powerful and fast shark, with a stocky body, a minute second dorsal and anal fin, and a lunate caudal fin. It has a conical snout; large, deep green eyes; and smooth, long, slender teeth. Coloring on the upper body is a grayish blue to charcoal and the lower body is white. There is a white spot at the base of the first dorsal fin.

REPRODUCTION The species is ovoviviparous and oophagous (see page 80), giving birth to 1–5 pups per litter.

COMMENT One of the smallest of the mackerel sharks, the porbeagle is often mistaken for the shortfin mako. It has suffered from overfishing, particularly in the North Atlantic, and numbers have fallen dramatically.

BROWN CATSHARK *Apristurus brunneus*

Not to scale

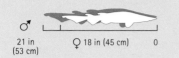

♂
21 in
(53 cm)   ♀ 18 in (45 cm)   0

- OTHER NAMES: None
- SIZE AT BIRTH: 3 inches (7.5 cm)
- MAXIMUM LENGTH: 2¼ feet (68 cm)
- DIET: Pelagic shrimp, squid, and small fishes
- HABITAT: Continental shelves and slopes from 100–3,000 feet (30–900 m), well above the bottom
- DISTRIBUTION: British Columbia to Baja California

APPEARANCE The brown catshark has a long, slender body, with two dorsal fins of similar size, small pectoral fins, and a long anal fin that reaches to the start of the elongate caudal fin. This harmless species has small eyes with nictitating membranes, small teeth, relatively large gill slits, and a long, broad snout. Coloring is chocolate brown on the upper body and underside, with pale fin margins.

REPRODUCTION The brown catshark is oviparous, laying one egg at a time in a 2 inch (5 cm) long case. It is believed that they hatch after about 12 months.

COMMENT Although quite a common deep-water shark, little is known about the brown catshark or any of the other species in the genus *Apristurus*. Attempts have been made to keep the species in captivity, but with no success.

SWELLSHARK *Cephaloscyllium ventriosum*

Not to scale

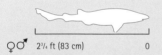

♀♂   2¾ ft (83 cm)   0

- OTHER NAMES: None
- SIZE AT BIRTH: 5½ in (14 cm)
- MAXIMUM LENGTH: 3½ feet (1 m)
- DIET: Bottom fishes
- HABITAT: Beneath and around kelp beds associated with reefs from depths of 30–200 feet (10–60 m)
- DISTRIBUTION: Temperate eastern Pacific, from California to Mexico and central Chile

APPEARANCE
One of the largest catsharks, the nocturnal swellshark is a relatively sluggish species with a stout body, two dorsal fins set toward the rear of the body, an anal fin that is larger than the small second dorsal fin, and a long caudal fin. It has prickly skin, a flattened head, broadly rounded snout, elongate eyes with nictitating membranes, and a large mouth filled with numerous small, pointed teeth. Coloring is yellowish brown to brown, with brown blotches and black dots all over the body. Juveniles are lighter in color, darkening as they age.

REPRODUCTION
The species is oviparous, laying two eggs at a time in amber, tendril-covered cases. These hatch in 7–10 months.

COMMENT To protect against predators, the swellshark wedges itself between rocks by swallowing large amounts of water to inflate its stomach up to three times its normal size.

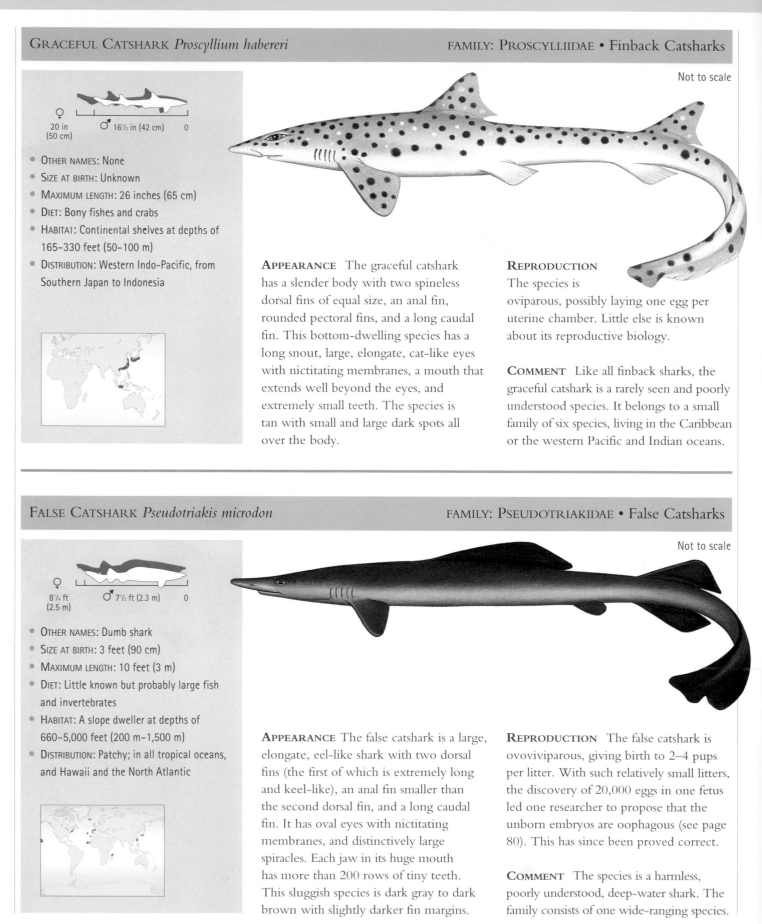

GRACEFUL CATSHARK *Proscyllium habereri*

FAMILY: PROSCYLLIIDAE • Finback Catsharks

Not to scale

♀ 20 in (50 cm)   ♂ 16½ in (42 cm)   0

- OTHER NAMES: None
- SIZE AT BIRTH: Unknown
- MAXIMUM LENGTH: 26 inches (65 cm)
- DIET: Bony fishes and crabs
- HABITAT: Continental shelves at depths of 165–330 feet (50–100 m)
- DISTRIBUTION: Western Indo-Pacific, from Southern Japan to Indonesia

APPEARANCE The graceful catshark has a slender body with two spineless dorsal fins of equal size, an anal fin, rounded pectoral fins, and a long caudal fin. This bottom-dwelling species has a long snout, large, elongate, cat-like eyes with nictitating membranes, a mouth that extends well beyond the eyes, and extremely small teeth. The species is tan with small and large dark spots all over the body.

REPRODUCTION The species is oviparous, possibly laying one egg per uterine chamber. Little else is known about its reproductive biology.

COMMENT Like all finback sharks, the graceful catshark is a rarely seen and poorly understood species. It belongs to a small family of six species, living in the Caribbean or the western Pacific and Indian oceans.

FALSE CATSHARK *Pseudotriakis microdon*

FAMILY: PSEUDOTRIAKIDAE • False Catsharks

Not to scale

♀ 8¼ ft (2.5 m)   ♂ 7½ ft (2.3 m)   0

- OTHER NAMES: Dumb shark
- SIZE AT BIRTH: 3 feet (90 cm)
- MAXIMUM LENGTH: 10 feet (3 m)
- DIET: Little known but probably large fish and invertebrates
- HABITAT: A slope dweller at depths of 660–5,000 feet (200 m–1,500 m)
- DISTRIBUTION: Patchy; in all tropical oceans, and Hawaii and the North Atlantic

APPEARANCE The false catshark is a large, elongate, eel-like shark with two dorsal fins (the first of which is extremely long and keel-like), an anal fin smaller than the second dorsal fin, and a long caudal fin. It has oval eyes with nictitating membranes, and distinctively large spiracles. Each jaw in its huge mouth has more than 200 rows of tiny teeth. This sluggish species is dark gray to dark brown with slightly darker fin margins.

REPRODUCTION The false catshark is ovoviviparous, giving birth to 2–4 pups per litter. With such relatively small litters, the discovery of 20,000 eggs in one fetus led one researcher to propose that the unborn embryos are oophagous (see page 80). This has since been proved correct.

COMMENT The species is a harmless, poorly understood, deep-water shark. The family consists of one wide-ranging species.

BARBELED HOUNDSHARK *Leptocharias smithii*

FAMILY: LEPTOCHARIIDAE • Barbeled Houndsharks

Not to scale

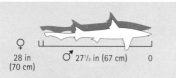

♀ 28 in (70 cm)   ♂ 27½ in (67 cm)   0

- OTHER NAMES: None
- SIZE AT BIRTH: 1 foot (30 cm)
- MAXIMUM LENGTH: 2¾ feet (83 cm)
- DIET: Bottom-living crustaceans, small fishes, and floating fish eggs
- HABITAT: Bottom dweller at depths of 33–250 feet (10 m–75 m)
- DISTRIBUTION: West Africa from Mauritania to Angola

APPEARANCE The only species in the family, the barbeled houndshark is a small shark with a slender, tapering body. It has two spineless dorsal fins (the second being significantly smaller than the first), an anal fin only slightly smaller than the second dorsal, and a long caudal fin. It has a small head, a long mouth, slender barbels, large eyes, and small spiracles. Coloring is light grey to brown and paler on the underside.

REPRODUCTION The barbeled houndshark is viviparous, giving birth to about seven pups per litter after a minimum gestation period of four months.

COMMENT Males have larger teeth than females, possibly for grasping the females during copulation. The species is an omnivorous scavenger and all sorts of inedible objects, including feathers and flowers, have been found in its stomach.

SOUPFIN SHARK *Galeorhinus galeus*

FAMILY: TRIAKIDAE • Houndsharks

Not to scale

♀ 5¼ ft (1.6 m)   ♂ 5 ft (1.5 m)   0

- OTHER NAMES: Tope shark, school shark, vitamin shark, snapper shark
- SIZE AT BIRTH: 1 foot (30 cm)
- MAXIMUM LENGTH: 6½ feet (2 m)
- DIET: Mostly bony fishes, but also squid and octopus
- HABITAT: Coastal, on bottom from shallow water to 1,800 feet (550 m)
- DISTRIBUTION: Widespread in Pacific and Atlantic oceans, Mediterranean Sea, southern Australia, and New Zealand

APPEARANCE An active shark that spends most of its time swimming, the soupfin shark has quite a slender body with two dorsal fins, the second of which is significantly smaller than the first and about the same size as the anal fin. The large lobe on the caudal fin gives it the unusual appearance of a double tail. It has a long snout and elongate eyes with nictitating eyelids. Coloring is bronze gray with a pale underside.

REPRODUCTION This species is ovoviviparous, giving birth in shallow waters in spring and early summer after a gestation period of one year. Litters vary from 15–50 pups with the larger females bearing the larger litters.

COMMENT The soupfin shark makes long migrations, possibly for purposes of reproduction. The flesh, fins, and liver of this shark are much sought after for human consumption, and many fisheries have collapsed due to overfishing.

DUSKY SMOOTHHOUND *Mustelus canis*

FAMILY: TRIAKIDAE • Houndsharks

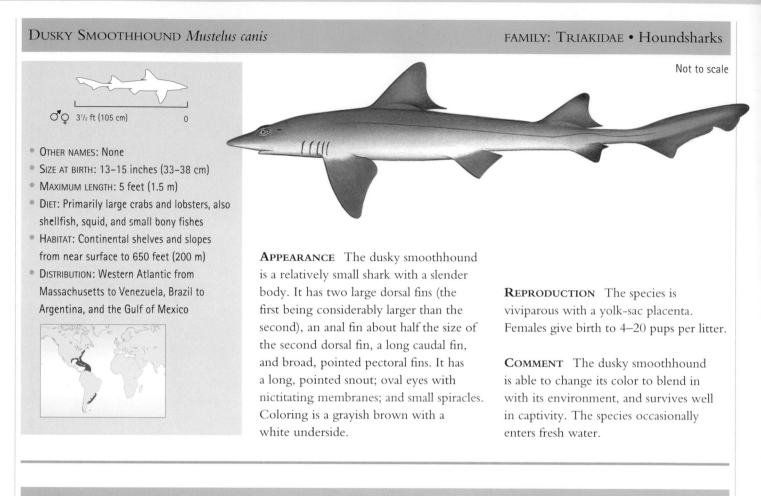

Not to scale

♂♀ 3½ ft (105 cm)   0

- OTHER NAMES: None
- SIZE AT BIRTH: 13–15 inches (33–38 cm)
- MAXIMUM LENGTH: 5 feet (1.5 m)
- DIET: Primarily large crabs and lobsters, also shellfish, squid, and small bony fishes
- HABITAT: Continental shelves and slopes from near surface to 650 feet (200 m)
- DISTRIBUTION: Western Atlantic from Massachusetts to Venezuela, Brazil to Argentina, and the Gulf of Mexico

APPEARANCE The dusky smoothhound is a relatively small shark with a slender body. It has two large dorsal fins (the first being considerably larger than the second), an anal fin about half the size of the second dorsal fin, a long caudal fin, and broad, pointed pectoral fins. It has a long, pointed snout; oval eyes with nictitating membranes; and small spiracles. Coloring is a grayish brown with a white underside.

REPRODUCTION The species is viviparous with a yolk-sac placenta. Females give birth to 4–20 pups per litter.

COMMENT The dusky smoothhound is able to change its color to blend in with its environment, and survives well in captivity. The species occasionally enters fresh water.

LEOPARD SHARK *Triakis semifasciata*

FAMILY: TRIAKIDAE • Houndsharks

Not to scale

♀ 5 ft (1.5 m)   ♂ 4 ft (1.2 m)   0

- OTHER NAMES: None
- SIZE AT BIRTH: 8 inches (20 cm)
- MAXIMUM LENGTH: 7 feet (2.1 m)
- DIET: Bony fishes, fish eggs, crustaceans, and worms
- HABITAT: Shallow bays and shallow open coastal waters
- DISTRIBUTION: Oregon to Baja California

APPEARANCE The leopard shark is a sluggish species with a medium-sized, elongate body. It has two dorsal fins of similar size, pointed pectoral fins, an anal fin that is smaller than the second dorsal fin, and an asymmetrical caudal fin. The shark has oval eyes with nictitating membranes, a long snout, small spiracles, and small, pointed teeth. Coloring is bronze to golden brown with dark saddles and black spots. Some individuals may have stripes as well as spots on their bodies.

REPRODUCTION The species is ovoviviparous, without a yolk-sac placenta. The female gives birth in coastal bays to 4–29 pups per litter in spring after a gestation period of one year.

COMMENT Harmless to humans, the leopard shark is often mistaken for the dangerous tiger shark. It survives well in captivity.

ATLANTIC WEASEL SHARK *Paragaleus pectoralis*

FAMILY: HEMIGALEIDAE • Weasel Sharks

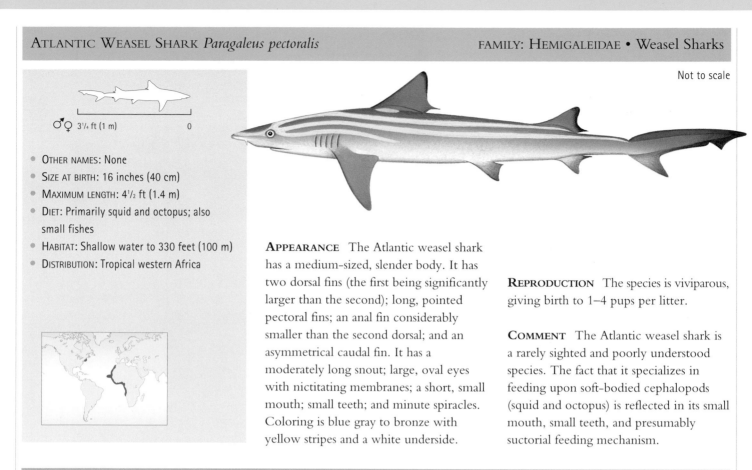

Not to scale

♂♀ 3¼ ft (1 m)　　　　0

- OTHER NAMES: None
- SIZE AT BIRTH: 16 inches (40 cm)
- MAXIMUM LENGTH: 4½ ft (1.4 m)
- DIET: Primarily squid and octopus; also small fishes
- HABITAT: Shallow water to 330 feet (100 m)
- DISTRIBUTION: Tropical western Africa

APPEARANCE The Atlantic weasel shark has a medium-sized, slender body. It has two dorsal fins (the first being significantly larger than the second); long, pointed pectoral fins; an anal fin considerably smaller than the second dorsal; and an asymmetrical caudal fin. It has a moderately long snout; large, oval eyes with nictitating membranes; a short, small mouth; small teeth; and minute spiracles. Coloring is blue gray to bronze with yellow stripes and a white underside.

REPRODUCTION The species is viviparous, giving birth to 1–4 pups per litter.

COMMENT The Atlantic weasel shark is a rarely sighted and poorly understood species. The fact that it specializes in feeding upon soft-bodied cephalopods (squid and octopus) is reflected in its small mouth, small teeth, and presumably suctorial feeding mechanism.

SILVERTIP SHARK *Carcharhinus albimarginatus*

FAMILY: CARCHARHINIDAE • Requiem Sharks

Not to scale

♂♀ 10 ft (3 m)　　　　0

- OTHER NAMES: Silvertip whaler
- SIZE AT BIRTH: 2⅛ feet (65 cm)
- MAXIMUM LENGTH: 10 feet (3 m)
- DIET: Pelagic and bottom fishes
- HABITAT: Along reef dropoffs from the surface to 2,625 feet (800 m)
- DISTRIBUTION: Widespread in tropical Indo-Pacific; east coast of Africa from the Red Sea and South Africa eastward to the eastern Pacific and Mexico to Columbia

APPEARANCE The silvertip shark has a stocky body; two dorsal fins (the first being significantly larger than the second); long, pointed pectoral fins; an anal fin; and an asymmetrical caudal fin. It has a moderately long, rounded snout; round eyes; and no spiracles. The upper body is bronze and the underside is pale. This shark is easily recognized by the white tips on its pectoral, pelvic, caudal, and first dorsal fins. The anal and second dorsal fins are unmarked.

REPRODUCTION The species is viviparous. After a gestation period of 12 months, the female gives birth to 5–6 young, although sometimes there are as few as 1 or as many as 11 pups per litter.

COMMENT Although there have been few reports of attacks, the silvertip shark is potentially dangerous and divers should be extremely cautious.

GRAY REEF SHARK *Carcharhinus amblyrhynchos*   FAMILY: CARCHARHINIDAE • Requiem Sharks

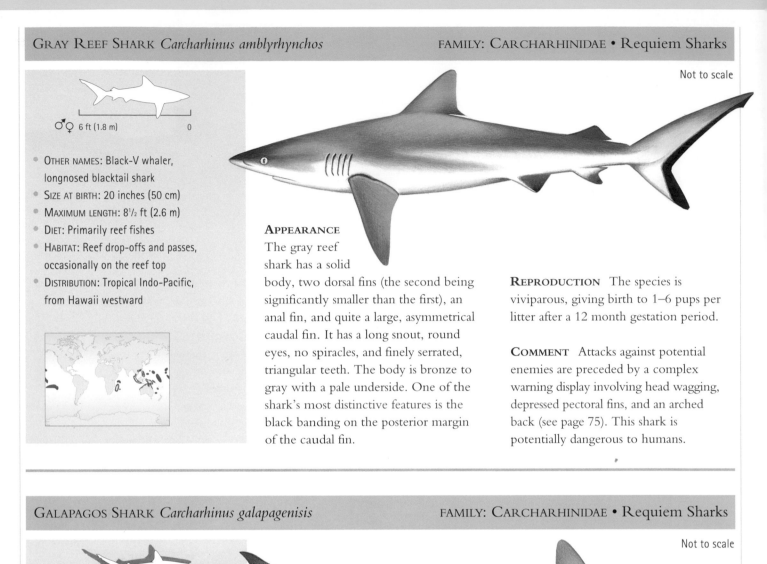

Not to scale

♂♀ 6 ft (1.8 m)   0

- OTHER NAMES: Black-V whaler, longnosed blacktail shark
- SIZE AT BIRTH: 20 inches (50 cm)
- MAXIMUM LENGTH: 8¹/₂ ft (2.6 m)
- DIET: Primarily reef fishes
- HABITAT: Reef drop-offs and passes, occasionally on the reef top
- DISTRIBUTION: Tropical Indo-Pacific, from Hawaii westward

APPEARANCE

The gray reef shark has a solid body, two dorsal fins (the second being significantly smaller than the first), an anal fin, and quite a large, asymmetrical caudal fin. It has a long snout, round eyes, no spiracles, and finely serrated, triangular teeth. The body is bronze to gray with a pale underside. One of the shark's most distinctive features is the black banding on the posterior margin of the caudal fin.

REPRODUCTION The species is viviparous, giving birth to 1–6 pups per litter after a 12 month gestation period.

COMMENT Attacks against potential enemies are preceded by a complex warning display involving head wagging, depressed pectoral fins, and an arched back (see page 75). This shark is potentially dangerous to humans.

GALAPAGOS SHARK *Carcharhinus galapagenisis*   FAMILY: CARCHARHINIDAE • Requiem Sharks

Not to scale

♀ 9 ft (2.7 m)   ♂ 7¹/₂ ft (2.3 m)   0

- OTHER NAMES: None
- SIZE AT BIRTH: 23–32 inches (57–80 cm)
- MAXIMUM LENGTH: 12 feet (3.6 m)
- DIET: Reef fishes
- HABITAT: Just beyond outer reef edge
- DISTRIBUTION: Cosmopolitan in tropics, generally near oceanic islands

APPEARANCE This is a typical requiem shark with a stocky body and a low but prominent ridge between the dorsal fins. However, it lacks the conspicuous white or black markings on the fins. The Galapagos shark has large pectoral fins with narrow, rounded tips; a high first dorsal fin; and a second dorsal fin that is similar in size to the anal fin. It has a long, rounded snout; round eyes; and no spiracles. The body is charcoal gray to brown with a pale, almost white underside, and most of the fins have dusky tips that fade with age.

REPRODUCTION The species is viviparous, giving birth in shallow waters to 6–16 pups per litter.

COMMENT Although the Galapagos shark has attacked humans, it is generally not considered to be dangerous.

BULL SHARK *Carcharhinus leucas*

FAMILY: CARCHARHINIDAE • Requiem Sharks

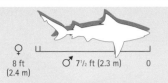

♀ 8 ft (2.4 m)   ♂ 7½ ft (2.3 m)   0

- OTHER NAMES: Lake Nicaragua shark, fresh-water whaler, Zambezi shark
- SIZE AT BIRTH: 22–32 inches (55–80 cm)
- MAXIMUM LENGTH: 11½ ft (3.5 m)
- DIET: Omnivorous, eating turtles, birds, dolphins, crustaceans, and cephalopods, but preferring bony fishes and other sharks
- HABITAT: Estuaries, rivers, and coastal waters to 100 feet (30 m)
- DISTRIBUTION: All tropical and subtropical seas

Not to scale

APPEARANCE

The bull shark has a heavy body, broad pectoral fins with pointed tips, and two dorsal fins (the first being significantly larger than the second). It lacks the interdorsal ridge and distinctive fin markings typical of requiem sharks. It has large jaws; triangular, sharp, serrated teeth; round eyes; and no spiracles. The species is so named because of the broad, rounded snout that gives it the appearance of a bull. Coloring is gray with a white underside, and juveniles have dark tips on their fins.

REPRODUCTION
The species is viviparous, mating in late spring and summer, and giving birth in shallow waters to 1–13 pups per litter after a gestation period of 10–11 months.

COMMENT
An extremely dangerous species, it has attacked and killed humans in all oceans as well as in fresh-water rivers and lakes.

OCEANIC WHITETIP SHARK *Carcharhinus longimanus*

FAMILY: CARCHARHINIDAE • Requiem Sharks

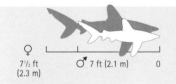

♀ 7½ ft (2.3 m)   ♂ 7 ft (2.1 m)   0

- OTHER NAMES: Whitetip whaler, whitetip shark
- SIZE AT BIRTH: 2½ feet (75 cm)
- MAXIMUM LENGTH: 13 feet (4 m)
- DIET: Wide ranging, including fishes, squid, birds, turtles, and carrion
- HABITAT: Offshore, from the surface to 500 feet (150 m)
- DISTRIBUTION: All tropical and subtropical seas

Not to scale

APPEARANCE
A large shark, the oceanic whitetip has a stocky body, two dorsal fins (the first being extremely large and rounded), long pectoral fins, and a low interdorsal ridge. It has a short, broad, rounded snout; triangular, sharp, serrated teeth; round eyes; and no spiracles. The upper body is brownish gray fading to white on the underside. The rounded tips of the first dorsal fin and the pectoral fins, and often the tip of the lower lobe of the caudal fin, are white.

REPRODUCTION
The species is viviparous, giving birth to 6–15 pups per litter after a gestation period of 12 months.

COMMENT
The oceanic whitetip is dangerous to humans. Although it is usually a slow swimmer, it can swim quickly in short bursts.

BLACKTIP REEF SHARK *Carcharhinus melanopterus*

FAMILY: CARCHARHINIDAE • Requiem Sharks

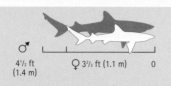

♂ 4½ ft (1.4 m) ♀ 3⅔ ft (1.1 m) 0

- OTHER NAMES: Blacktip shark, guliman
- SIZE AT BIRTH: 20 inches (50 cm)
- MAXIMUM LENGTH: 6 feet (1.8 m)
- DIET: Primarily reef fishes, but also crustaceans and cephalopods
- HABITAT: Shallow reef flats to outer reef edge
- DISTRIBUTION: Tropical central Pacific to eastern Africa; entered the Mediterranean through Suez Canal

Not to scale

APPEARANCE The blacktip reef shark is a small to medium-sized shark with a thick body, two dorsal fins (the second significantly shorter than the first), an anal fin, an asymmetrical caudal fin, and no interdorsal ridge. It has large eyes, lacks spiracles, and has a short, rounded snout. This shark is yellowish brown to gray, with a paler strip on the flanks and a white underside. The most distinctive feature of the species is that all fins have black tips, the most noticeable being those on the first dorsal and lower caudal fins.

REPRODUCTION The species is viviparous, giving birth in shallow waters to 2–4 pups per litter after a gestation of 8–9 months.

COMMENT While not considered dangerous to divers, the blacktip reef shark has been known to bite reef walkers, probably attracted by their splashing.

TIGER SHARK *Galeocerdo cuvier*

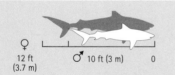

♀ 12 ft (3.7 m) ♂ 10 ft (3 m) 0

- OTHER NAMES: None
- SIZE AT BIRTH: 20-30 inches (50-75 cm)
- MAXIMUM LENGTH: 24 feet (7.3 m)
- DIET: Extremely wide ranging, including turtles, fishes, seals, birds, carrion, and virtually anything that falls overboard
- HABITAT: Inshore along coral and rocky reefs at night and beyond the reef edge to 500 feet (150 m) in daytime
- DISTRIBUTION: Worldwide in tropics

APPEARANCE The tiger shark has a large, stout body that tapers to a well-developed, long, pointed caudal fin. It has a large, flattened head; a large, blunt nose; a wide mouth; small spiracles located just behind the eyes; and 18 to 20 rows of sharp, asymmetrical, finely serrated teeth in each jaw that enable it to eat virtually anything it pleases. Coloration of the upper body is bluish gray to brown and the underside is yellow to light grey or white. The tiger shark is so named because the body is covered

LEMON SHARK *Negaprion brevirostris*

Not to scale

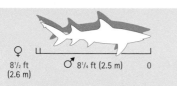

♀ 8½ ft (2.6 m)   ♂ 8¼ ft (2.5 m)   0

- OTHER NAMES: None
- SIZE AT BIRTH: 2 feet (60 cm)
- MAXIMUM LENGTH: 11 feet (3.4 m)
- DIET: Bony fishes, rays, crustaceans, and mollusks
- HABITAT: Shallow seagrass beds and mangrove flats
- DISTRIBUTION: Western Atlantic from New Jersey to Brazil, possibly eastern Atlantic, and eastern Pacific from Baja California to Ecuador

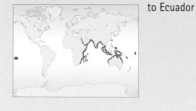

APPEARANCE The lemon shark is a sluggish species with a stocky body, two large dorsal fins (the second being almost as large as the first), a large anal fin, and broad pectoral fins. It has a broad, flattened head; a short nose; smooth, dagger-like teeth; and occasionally vestigial spiracles. Coloring is pale yellow, light brown, or mustard fading to a lemon yellow or white on the underside.

REPRODUCTION The species is viviparous, mating in spring and summer. After a gestation period of up to 14 months (in warmer temperatures the gestation period is shorter), females give birth in shallow waters to 4–17 pups per litter.

COMMENT The lemon shark is harmless unless provoked. Much research has been carried out on the species as it survives well in captivity.

Not to scale

with black or dark gray vertical stripes that fade with maturity.

REPRODUCTION The only ovoviviparous requiem shark, the tiger shark gives birth to 10–82 pups per litter after a gestation period of 12–13 months.

COMMENT Believed to be nocturnal, the tiger shark is extremely dangerous, having attacked and consumed human swimmers in all seas. Although it is usually a slow swimmer, it can move quickly in short spurts and regularly enters very shallow waters.

BLUE SHARK *Prionace glauca*

FAMILY: CARCHARHINIDAE • Requiem Sharks

♀
9¼ ft
(2.8 m)   ♂ 8¼ ft (2.5 m)   0

- OTHER NAMES: Blue whaler, great blue shark, blue dog
- SIZE AT BIRTH: 16 inches (40 cm)
- MAXIMUM LENGTH: 12½ feet (3.9 m)
- DIET: Pelagic fishes, squid, and krill
- HABITAT: Oceanic, from the surface to 1,150 feet (350 m), and close to shore in some locations
- DISTRIBUTION: All tropical and temperate seas

Not to scale

APPEARANCE One of the most easily recognizable species, the blue shark has a slender body with two dorsal fins, no interdorsal ridge, and long, narrow pectoral fins. It has a narrow head; a long, narrow snout; serrated, triangular teeth; and large eyes with a white rim. There are occasionally vestigial spiracles. Coloring is bright indigo blue on the upper body, paler on the flanks, and white on the underside.

REPRODUCTION The species is viviparous. Mating occurs in summer but the female retains the sperm until ovulation in the following spring. Then, after a gestation period of 9–12 months, she gives birth in the open ocean. Litter sizes vary from 4–135 with about 40 being the average.

COMMENT Once extremely common, the number of blue sharks has now been reduced worldwide due to overfishing. The species is dangerous to humans and will attack without provocation.

WHITETIP REEF SHARK *Triaenodon obesus*

FAMILY: CARCHARHINIDAE • Requiem Sharks

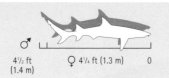

♂
4½ ft
(1.4 m)   ♀ 4¼ ft (1.3 m)   0

- OTHER NAMES: Blunthead shark
- SIZE AT BIRTH: 21–24 inches (52–60 cm)
- MAXIMUM LENGTH: 7 feet (2.1 m)
- DIET: Bottom fishes, crustaceans, and cephalopods
- HABITAT: A shallow-water reef dweller, to depths of 1,000 feet (300 m)
- DISTRIBUTION: Tropical eastern Pacific to eastern Africa, widespread in Oceania

Not to scale

APPEARANCE The whitetip reef shark has a slender body with two dorsal fins, the second of which is almost equal in size to the anal fin. The pectoral and dorsal fins have pointed tips, the head is broad, and the snout is short and rounded. There are occasionally vestigial spiracles. Coloring is gray to brown, fading to a pale underside, and dark blotches are sometimes splattered on the body. The first dorsal and upper caudal fins, and sometimes the second dorsal and lower caudal fins, have distinctive white tips.

REPRODUCTION The species is viviparous, giving birth to 1–5 pups per litter after a gestation period of 13 months.

COMMENT Most active at night, the whitetip reef shark is extremely curious. It is not dangerous to humans but is often attracted to the sounds made by divers.

SCALLOPED HAMMERHEAD *Sphyrna lewini* FAMILY: SPHYRNIDAE • Hammerhead Sharks

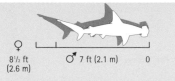

♀ 8½ ft (2.6 m)   ♂ 7 ft (2.1 m)   0

Not to scale

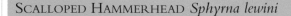

- **OTHER NAMES:** Kidney-headed shark, bronze hammerhead
- **SIZE AT BIRTH:** 17–22 inches (43–55 cm)
- **MAXIMUM LENGTH:** 12 feet (3.7 m), possibly larger
- **DIET:** Bony fishes and squid
- **HABITAT:** Coastal, from the surface to 900 feet (270 m)
- **DISTRIBUTION:** Worldwide in tropical and warm-temperate seas

APPEARANCE Hammerhead sharks are most easily recognized by the lateral extension of their head, with their nostrils and eyes located on the tips of the "hammer." They also have two dorsal fins, small pectoral fins, and an anal fin. This hammerhead has a distinctively curved forward margin on its head giving it a scalloped appearance. Coloring is deep olive green, brown, gray, or bronze and the pectoral fins often have charcoal gray to black tips.

REPRODUCTION The species is viviparous, with a yolk-sac placenta. Females give birth in shallow waters after a gestation period of 9–10 months. Litter sizes range from 15–30 pups, with the larger females having the larger litters.

COMMENT Probably the most abundant hammerhead shark, the scalloped hammerhead is often seen in large schools by divers in Hawaii, Galapagos, and Baja California. It is harmless to humans.

GREAT HAMMERHEAD *Sphyrna mokarran* FAMILY: SPHYRNIDAE • Hammerhead Sharks

Not to scale

♀ 12 ft (3.7 m)   ♂ 9½ ft (2.9 m)   0

- **OTHER NAMES:** Scoop hammerhead
- **SIZE AT BIRTH:** 2⅕ feet (65 cm)
- **MAXIMUM LENGTH:** 20 feet (6.1 m)
- **DIET:** Other sharks and rays
- **HABITAT:** Coastal and above continental shelves, from surface to 260 feet (80 m)
- **DISTRIBUTION:** All tropical seas; not found in Hawaii

APPEARANCE The great hammerhead has a moderately slender body, two dorsal fins (the first of which is quite high), and an anal fin. The species has a distinctive hammer-shaped head, which is straight at the front margin except for one indentation in the middle, with the nostrils and eyes on the tips of the hammer. Coloring is a bronze to grayish brown or dark olive, and the underside is lighter.

REPRODUCTION The species is viviparous, giving birth in late spring to summer after an 11 month gestation period. Litter sizes range from 6–33, with the larger females having the larger litters.

COMMENT Although most hammerhead species are harmless to humans, the great hammerhead is an exception and has attacked on occasion.

SHARKS AND PEOPLE

THROUGH THE AGES, SHARKS HAVE PLAYED A
PART IN ART, RELIGION, AND MYTHOLOGY.
WHILE THERE IS A COMMON MISCONCEPTION
THAT ALL SHARKS ARE POTENTIAL KILLERS,
IT IS IN FACT HUMANKIND THAT IS
THREATENING THE SURVIVAL OF SHARKS.
IT IS ONLY THROUGH CONTINUED RESEARCH
THAT WE CAN FULLY UNDERSTAND AND
RESPECT THESE AMAZING CREATURES.

THE SHARK IN ART, MYTH, AND LEGEND

Despite being much maligned and largely misunderstood, sharks appear in the art and mythology of many cultures, and have done so for thousands of years. Sharks feature most prominently in the myths and legends of sea-based cultures. People whose lives were closely associated with the sea encountered sharks often and treated them with a combination of fear and reverence. In the West, where contact with sharks has been less frequent, these creatures have generally been seen in narrow terms, as malevolent, single-minded predators.

ABOVE: *This carving from the Santa Cruz Islands in the South Pacific depicts a shark god in human form. Local fishermen once worshiped this image for luck before hunting sharks.*

SHARKS AND SEA-BASED CULTURES

Virtually all cultures with strong ties to the sea incorporate the shark into their art and mythology. Around the Pacific Ocean, people have been drawing and carving sharks on rocks and wood for centuries. On North America's Pacific coast, Tlingit people used shark crests as the emblems for tribal clans, and in Central and South America, shark images and scenes of shark attacks appear on ancient pottery.

Sharks feature prominently among the gods worshiped by Pacific cultures. Until the 19th century, natives of the Cook Islands worshiped the shark-god Tiaio, and in the Solomon Islands, a shark-god known as *tak manacca* was placated with human sacrifices. Sharks also appear in many creation stories from the region. According to one Australian Aboriginal story, the oceans and rivers were created by a large sawshark. Aboriginal mythology also tells how the tiger shark Bangudja attacked a dolphin-man in the Gulf of Carpentaria, leaving a red stain still visible on the rocks of Chasm Island.

Sharks play a central role in many Polynesian myths and legends. In Hawaii, it was believed that "shark-men," or *mano kanaka*, would emerge from the water to follow swimmers

ABOVE: *This rock painting of a shark was made by Aborigines in northern Australia. Sharks are plentiful in the warm waters off the north Australian coast and they feature in a number of Aboriginal creation myths.*

RIGHT: *The importance of the sea to the Roman Empire is reflected in the number of murals depicting sea creatures that date from Roman times. This mural from the second century AD was found in Tunisia and shows Neptune, the god of the sea, surrounded by various sea creatures. These include a reasonably accurate depiction of a ray.*

and fishermen, later turning back into sharks to devour them. According to one such legend from Hawaii, a shark-man called Kapa'aheo was killed by locals, whereupon he turned into a large, shark-shaped rock. This rock can be seen today in Honolulu's Bishop Museum.

Both Hawaiians and Tahitians believe that a relative can return after death in the form of a shark to act as a guardian. Tahitians believe that such ancestor sharks can be asked to settle arguments or avenge one's honor—a superstition that has been blamed for the widespread reluctance of Tahitian spearfishermen to work at sea after fights with their wives!

Such superstitions about sharks are common among sea-based communities. In eastern Africa, boat builders still anoint new hulls with oil extracted from hammerhead sharks to bring good luck to the crew. Recently in Hawaii, when the United States Navy planned to build a dry-dock at Pearl Harbor, locals objected, explaining that a cave beneath the site was the home of the son of a legendary guardian shark. Construction went ahead regardless; but interestingly, when the dry-dock was almost completed, it collapsed and all work was lost.

BELOW: The Greek historian Herodotus was one of the first writers to see the dramatic potential of sharks, describing in vivid detail how shipwrecked Persian soldiers were attacked and killed by sharks in waters off the island of Athos in 492 BC.

SHARKS IN THE WESTERN WORLD

For most Western cultures, the sea has had a less immediate influence on everyday life, and as a result, sharks are not prominent in Western art or mythology. However, references have occurred from time to time since antiquity.

There are images of sharks in ancient Roman mosaics and in the literature of both the ancient Greeks and Romans. In about 330 BC, Aristotle wrote about sharks in great detail in his *Historia Animalium*. He accurately described the distinction between the bony fishes and sharks, and gathered sharks and rays together into a group called *Selache*, a term still used by modern ichthyologists. Aristotle also began one of the most enduring myths about sharks—that they must turn upside down to bite. This misconception was still appearing in text books as recently as the 1940s.

While Aristotle turned a scholarly eye to sharks, other early writers focused on their fearsome nature, a preoccupation that endures to this day. In the fifth century BC, the Greek historian Herodotus described how shipwrecked Persian sailors were devoured by sharks, which he referred to as "monsters." Shark attacks also

ABOVE: *This 1778 painting by John Copley depicts the attack of Brook Watson in Havana Harbor 30 years earlier. Watson lost a leg in the attack, but went on to become a powerful figure in English politics. Well aware of the potent symbolism of his miraculous survival, he often exploited the episode in later life.*

captured the imagination of the Roman naturalist Pliny the Elder. Writing in his *Historia Naturalis* in about 77 BC, he vividly described how sharks attacked sponge divers in the Mediterranean Sea. He did note, however, that the sharks appeared to be just as afraid of the divers as the divers were of them.

Medieval European engravings and paintings of sea monsters include mythical beasts that bear a strong resemblance to sharks, and sailors'

journals often described menacing encounters with sharks. In 1555, Swedish historian Olaus Magnus described how malevolent "sea-dogfish" would attack swimmers and drag them to the bottom of the sea.

LEFT: *Medieval writers, such as Swedish historian Olaus Magnus, apparently based their depictions of sharks and other marine creatures on the notoriously unreliab... recollections of sea-farers. This sea monster from one... Magnus' newsletters in 15... may have been inspired by ... sailor's description of a sha...*

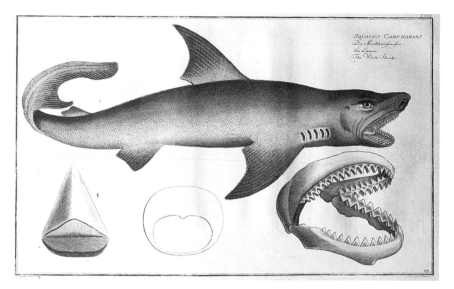

ABOVE: *Between 1785 and 1795, the German ichthyologist Marcus Bloch compiled detailed descriptions of the 15 shark species then recognized for his* Complete Natural History of Fish. *As influential as this work was, his illustrations contain many inaccuracies. In addition to having inverted jaws and misshapen fins, this so-called white shark appears to have been mistakenly based on a description of a requiem shark—probably a bull shark.*

RIGHT: *Steven Spielberg's* Jaws *contributed to a wave of anti-shark sentiment in the seventies. Interestingly, the "star" of the movie, a white shark, was embellished for this poster with the addition of an improbable set of mako-like teeth, perpetuating a long tradition of misrepresentation for this species.*

The characterization of sharks as shadowy, predatory monsters has been perpetuated in Western art and literature through the ages. The word "shark" may even derive from the German word "Schurke," meaning rascal, suggesting that the shark's bad reputation was established early. In English-speaking countries, the word has been used colloquially for centuries as a way to describe someone who is ruthless and efficient, as in the term "loan shark."

By the early 20th century, the shark was well established in the popular imagination as a malevolent, predatory force, and sharks were widely feared and loathed. There was a growing fascination with shark attacks, the lurid details of which often featured prominently in newspapers. During World War II, servicemen on both sides employed shark imagery to make their weapons appear even more menacing. German U-boat turrets were emblazoned with images of sawsharks, and shark jaws were often painted on United States fighter planes, a practice which continues to this day.

In 1974, public interest in sharks reached near-hysterical proportions with the release of the film based on Peter Benchley's book *Jaws.* This film distilled centuries of fascination, misconception, fear, and superstition regarding sharks into one potent symbol—a rogue great white shark, menacing a seaside community with ruthless efficiency in its single-minded pursuit of human flesh. For many people, this became the defining image of all sharks, despite the fact that the vast majority of species are harmless to humans.

THE SHARK TODAY

Since *Jaws,* the media obsession with shark attacks has been tempered by a growing awareness of the fascinating world in which sharks live and the many dangers they face from human interference. Improved technology has allowed greater access to sharks, and a number of recent books and films have increased our knowledge of their behavior and biology.

This is an important development in our understanding of sharks, and a vital one if sharks are to be protected from humans. While the popular Western image of the shark as an evil predator is powerful and entrenched, it remains a dangerous misconception. For as long as people see sharks in these terms, it is unlikely that they will appreciate the dangers these creatures face from overfishing and pollution.

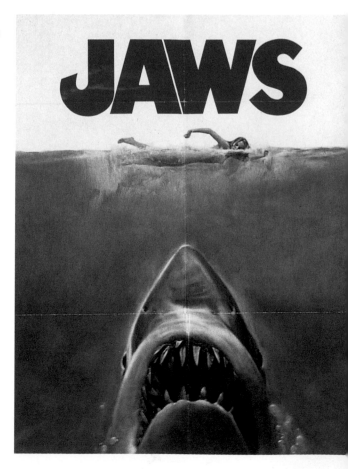

THE SHARK INDUSTRY

The demand for shark products is booming and nearly a million tons of shark are harvested annually by fisheries worldwide, both as targeted catch and as unintended bycatch. However, demand is beginning to outstrip supply, and overfishing threatens both the industry and the sharks themselves.

SHARK PRODUCTS

In the past, shark flesh was regarded by many Western consumers as inferior and even inedible, and was often marketed under alternative names, such as "rock salmon." Recently, however, shark meat (especially that of threshers and makos) has gained in popularity. Shark fin soup has been a Chinese delicacy for centuries, and the modern demand for shark fins has made them an extremely valuable commodity.

Virtually every part of a shark can be utilized. Historically, shark skin has been used as an abrasive and to decorate sword hilts and sheaths. Today, shark skin is considered a food delicacy by many Asian cultures, and it is used worldwide to make shoes, belts, handbags, and wallets. Shark teeth, traditionally used by Pacific Islanders to make tools and weapons, are still used today in tourist replicas of these weapons, as well as for jewelry. In the Philippines, people carve sharks from wood and fit them with real shark teeth.

Shark liver oil, once prized as a lubricant and source of vitamin A, has recently attracted interest for its pharmaceutical properties. Squalene, a compound found in the liver oil of deep-sea sharks, is used in pharmaceuticals, cosmetics, and as a lubricant in machinery.

There is a growing interest in the medicinal applications of shark products. Another property of shark liver oil, diacyl glycerol ether (DAGE), is used in the treatments of wounds and burns and a substance derived from shark cartilage is used as artificial skin for burn victims. Recently, shark corneas have been used for human corneal transplants.

FISHING METHODS

Sharks are captured using a variety of fishing methods, according to the species targeted and the habitat in which they live. Coastal sharks are most often captured with gillnets set on the seabed or with longlines. Gillnets form an invisible barrier into which the shark swims, becoming either gilled (caught by the head and gills) or entangled by the fins and body. Longlines consist of a mainline with multiple branch lines along its length, each of which ends in a baited hook. To capture open-ocean sharks, longlines or gillnets are set in waters close to the surface.

Some small schooling sharks, such as spiny dogfish and soupfin sharks, are captured by trawling giant mesh bags over the seabed to scoop them up. Deep-water trawl fisheries targeting fishes such as orange roughy, often unintentionally catch substantial numbers of deep-water sharks.

The two largest shark species, basking and whale sharks, are sometimes captured by small-scale traditional fisheries using harpoons. Large, acrobatic sharks, such as makos, are popular with sport fisheries, and anglers pay large sums for a chance to catch them.

LEFT: This exquisitely carved shark was made from wood in the Philippines and fitted with real shark teeth. Compared with the impact of large-scale fisheries, such traditional uses of shark products have little impact on shark numbers.

BELOW: There is a large market for shark products, such as shark liver oil and processed shark fins, especially in Asia. Such products are rapidly gaining popularity in the West, particularly for use as alternative medicines. Recently, shark cartilage has even been touted as a cure for cancer.

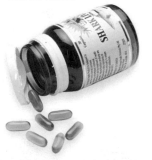

RIGHT: These sport fishermen are dragging a freshly caught lemon shark onto their boat. Growing public resistance to sport fishing has led the organizers of many shark-fishing competitions to institute a "no-kill" policy, whereby all captured sharks are returned to the sea.

BELOW: This hammerhead has been caught by the head and gills in a gillnet set on the seabed in waters off the Galapagos Islands. Such fishing practices are increasingly seen as unnecessarily cruel.

BOOM AND BUST

In the face of unrelenting demand, there are few convincing examples of a sustainable shark fishery on a modern, commercial scale. Virtually every shark fishery that has been established has initially boomed and then collapsed as a result of overfishing and poor management. The basking shark fishery of Achill Island off the coast of western Europe is a typical example. Between 1950 and 1955, a thousand or more sharks were landed each year. By the early 1960s, landings had decreased to fewer than a hundred sharks a year and the fishery crashed.

This pattern can also be seen in traditional fisheries. In the Philippines in the late 1980s, local people began fishing for whale sharks following the halting of traditional whaling operations. By the early 1990s, whale shark numbers had declined dramatically. Prices soared as a result and this in turn put increased pressure on the remaining whale shark stocks.

THREATS TO SHARKS

In the past decade there has been a dramatic increase in the number of sharks harvested throughout the world. Fishing pressure is by far the greatest threat facing shark populations, and even if consumer demand for shark products disappeared, an unsustainable number of sharks would continue to be killed as bycatch.

OVERFISHING

As early as 1974 biologists had recognized that sharks were susceptible to overfishing. Since then, despite growing worldwide evidence of overfishing, very few management plans or restrictions have been implemented in any country or region. Sadly, for many species of shark the best hope of long-term survival is that fishing becomes unprofitable before their numbers are reduced to unsustainable levels.

As recently as the 1970s the United States National Marine Fisheries Service was encouraging fishermen to turn to sharks as an "underutilized resource," and it spent large sums of money trying to convince consumers that shark flesh was an edible meat. Their efforts paid off, and shark fisheries rapidly developed in the 1980s. It wasn't until 1993, when shark populations off the Atlantic coast had been depleted by as much as 80 percent, that a management plan was finally implemented to reduce the fishing and finning of sharks, and to allow shark populations to recover.

Unfortunately, the same bleak scenario is repeated throughout most of the world. Of the 26 countries considered to be major harvesters of sharks, only three—the United States, New Zealand, and Australia—have

BELOW: A disturbing fishing practice of recent times is that of finning, whereby a shark's fins are cut off at sea, leaving the shark to die on the sea floor. The increasing demand for shark fins, particularly in parts of Asia where they are prized as both a delicacy and an aphrodisiac, has caused the price of fins to soar. As a result, sharks are increasingly targeted for their fins.

INSET: Shark fins drying on board a longline fishing boat.

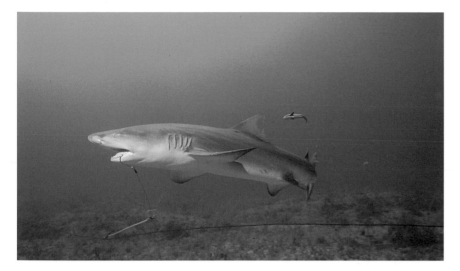

ABOVE: This lemon shark has been caught and killed on a longline in the Bahamas. Longlines are sometimes used to target sharks directly, but more often sharks are caught unintentionally on lines set up for tuna or swordfish.

shark management plans. Even these plans are limited in terms of the area they cover and the number of the species that are protected. Of the remaining countries, only South Africa, Canada, and the United Kingdom have any restrictions on shark fishing, and these are very limited, affecting as few as one or two species.

BYCATCH

A serious threat to shark populations, especially those inhabiting the open ocean, is that they are taken as bycatch in a wide variety of fisheries that target other fishes. Blue sharks, oceanic whitetips, thresher sharks, and other pelagic species are often caught on longlines set up to catch tuna and swordfish. In 1993, it was estimated that 8.3 million sharks were caught incidentally by swordfish and tuna fisheries worldwide. Many of these sharks were dead on the line and discarded at sea.

The devastating potential of the bycatch situation can be seen in the swordfish fishery operating off the east coast of Florida. During a two-year study between 1981 and 1983, not only did sharks constitute the largest part of the bycatch, but in most cases they actually exceeded the targeted swordfish catch.

A breakdown of sharks caught as bycatch demonstrates the serious threat that this situation poses to the long-term future of shark populations. In one study, it was found that 63 percent of sharks caught were females,

RIGHT: The sea is becoming an increasingly dangerous place for sharks, particularly those that frequent coastal waters. Here, a Port Jackson shark and an angelshark have been killed after becoming entangled in a discarded fishing net in waters off the east coast of Australia.

90 percent were immature and had never reproduced, and 66 percent were dead on the line. Such a high degree of mortality among females and juveniles of a species severely limits the rate at which a population can grow.

The greatest problem with bycatch fishing is that the number of sharks killed in this manner is often poorly documented. As sharks are not the target species, even a drastic decline in their catch rate will not affect the overall viability of a fishing operation and therefore will be generally ignored. Meanwhile, the shark populations continue to decline.

A particularly disturbing practice often associated with the bycatch of sharks is that of "finning." Shark fins are extremely valuable and take up very little room on fishing boats, so fishermen may cut the fins off sharks they have caught before dumping the bodies back in the oceans. Sharks are also directly targeted for their fins. They are caught on lines, finned, and then left to sink to the bottom of the ocean where they face a slow and painful death.

LACK OF FUNDING

One of the biggest problems facing attempts to manage shark fisheries is the relative economic insignificance of these fishing operations. While the increasing demand for shark products, particularly fins, has made it worthwhile for fishermen to actively target sharks, their economic significance is still tiny relative to other fishes. In 1997, thresher shark was selling for only US$1.50 a pound (US$0.68/kg), while swordfish was worth as much as US$5.00 a pound (US$2.25/kg). As a result, government agencies and commercial fishing operations are reluctant to fund research into shark exploitation, and little effort is put into remedying the bycatch problem.

OTHER THREATS TO SHARKS

Human encroachment into shark habitats is potentially as devastating to shark populations as commercial overfishing. A reason for this is that those habitats closest to areas of human concentration are among the most important

LEFT: These embryos were removed from a tiger shark that was captured and killed for its fins. Sharks are slow to reproduce and the death of a single female can have disastrous consequences for the sustainability of an entire population. Of the 26 countries considered to be major producers of shark products, more than a third have seen significant declines in shark populations and catch rates over the past few years.

ABOVE: This bay in Fiji has been heavily polluted by agricultural runoff following heavy rain. Unfortunately for sharks, sheltered bays such as this are favored nursery areas, and increasing pollution is threatening the viability of many shark populations.

to the viability of shark populations. For example, many sharks utilize protected embayments and estuaries as nursery areas. Scientists believe that these areas provide abundant food in the absence of predators, allowing young sharks to grow and develop in relative safety. When these sharks reach a larger size and become better hunters, they are less likely to be eaten and can safely move out of the nursery area.

Because of the proximity of many of these nursery areas to coastal towns and cities, they are susceptible to overfishing, as well as degradation from development and pollution. Clearly, the protection of adult sharks will not be effective unless the nursery areas used by their young also receive adequate protection. Recently, belated awareness of the importance of inshore nursery grounds to the sustainability of shark populations has led to increased

protection in certain parts of the world. However, in the face of the continued development of coastal areas worldwide, there is still a great deal more to be done.

"SHARK CONTROL"

Sharks are also under pressure from shark eradication programs, implemented in some countries to protect people from shark attacks. These programs typically try to remove the threat of "dangerous" sharks, either by fishing for particular species or by installing large barriers or gillnets around beaches where attacks have been known to occur. Although such programs have become less popular in recent years due to conservation concerns and a lack of evidence that they are particularly effective in preventing attacks, they are still in operation in some areas and continue to take a heavy toll on shark populations.

SHARK ATTACK

LEFT: A surfer on the west shore of Oahu, Hawaii. In recent years, surfers have become the most frequently attacked group of water users in Hawaii, a dubious honor once held by swimmers. This reflects the increasing popularity of surfing, as well as the fact that surfers often remain in the water for long periods of time.

There have been reports of sharks attacking people since the time of the ancient Greeks, and there is nothing to suggest that such attacks have not been occurring for as long as people have been entering the water. Shark attacks are traditionally broken down into two main categories—provoked and unprovoked. Provoked attacks are usually cases of sharks defending themselves against deliberate or inadvertent human interference. While unfortunate, such attacks are not particularly surprising. Unprovoked attacks, on the other hand, occur unpredictably and still pose something of a mystery.

In 1958, at the instigation of the United States Navy, a panel of scientists began to compile a worldwide historic database of shark attacks. By 1996 this database was known as the International Shark Attack File and contained more than 1,800 confirmed shark attacks. Between 75 and 100 new cases are added to the file each year, of which fewer than 20 are fatal. Unfortunately, due to the difficulties of documenting attacks in developing countries, information worldwide remains patchy.

WHY DO SHARKS ATTACK?

Although there are many reasons why a shark might attack a human, most attacks are likely to involve one of two behaviors—defense or predation. It appears that certain sharks act aggressively when approached too closely, and attacks may occur when a diver or swimmer is perceived as a threat. Gray reef sharks, in

ABOVE: From below, this boogie-boarder resembles a large marine animal on the surface. Whether a shark would perceive this in the same way, however, is unclear. A feeding shark might examine any object on the surface.

particular, exhibit a distinctive agonistic display when they feel threatened, sometimes followed by a swift attack (see page 75).

Shark attacks are often attributed to feeding behavior, and sharks may be provoked by food stimuli in the water such as blood from speared fishes. One explanation that has been proposed for unprovoked attacks is that sharks mistake people splashing on the surface for their usual prey. However, it is open to debate whether or not a shark actually mistakes a person for a particular kind of prey. It may be enough that the person is at the surface of the water where many species find much of their food, whether it be fishes, marine mammals, or carrion.

Feeding and defense account for many attacks, but they do not explain them all. While we can look for common themes, we will never know all the circumstances influencing a shark's behavior leading up to a specific attack, and the full picture remains far from complete.

WHO IS MOST AT RISK?

Not surprisingly, the majority of shark attacks occur where people and sharks are most likely to come into contact. Shark attacks have been recorded between 58°N and 46°S latitude, equivalent to the positions of Scotland and New Zealand. However, the peaks in attacks occur between 32°N and 34°S latitude—the area most densely populated by both humans and sharks.

Per capita, the greatest recorded number of shark attacks have occurred in Australia, the United States, and South Africa. These countries all have extensive coastlines within the peak latitudes and have seasonally warm

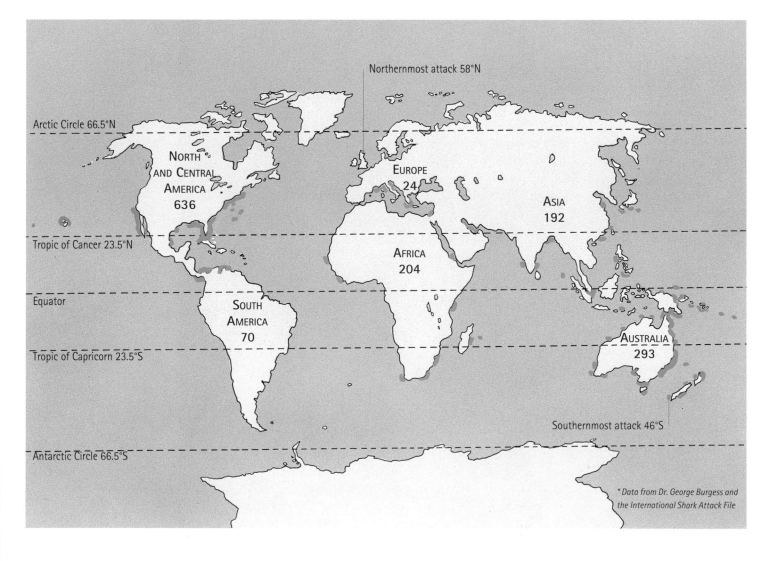

Northernmost attack 58°N

Arctic Circle 66.5°N

NORTH AND CENTRAL AMERICA 636

EUROPE 24

ASIA 192

Tropic of Cancer 23.5°N

AFRICA 204

Equator

SOUTH AMERICA 70

Tropic of Capricorn 23.5°S

AUSTRALIA 293

Southernmost attack 46°S

Antarctic Circle 66.5°S

*Data from Dr. George Burgess and the International Shark Attack File

water temperatures. Because the majority of shark attacks have occurred in these areas, it was once assumed that dangerous sharks prefer warm water. However, dangerous sharks are common in colder water too; it's just that people are less inclined to join them.

Most shark attacks occur close to shore, with approximately 31 percent of victims being within 50 feet (15 m) of the water's edge and 62 percent being in water that is less than 5 feet (1.5 m) deep. These figures are not surprising given that most people who enter the water do so as swimmers, surfers, and snorkelers, and seldom venture far offshore, while sharks frequently inhabit coastal areas.

Were people to swim in the open ocean, they would certainly be vulnerable to attack. This is confirmed by events such as the sinking of the *USS Indianapolis* at the end of World War II. Following a torpedo attack, the ship capsized, leaving around 800 men stranded in the tropical Pacific Ocean for nearly a week. During this time more than half of the men perished, and sharks are believed to have been responsible for as many as 100 of these deaths.

HOW FAR FROM SHORE DO ATTACKS OCCUR?

These figures, based on 570 attacks, provide a breakdown of attacks according to the victim's distance from shore. The figures in brackets show what percentage of people swim at these distances, indicating that attack statistics tell us nearly as much about the habits of people as they do about the habits of sharks.

* Data from Baldridge (1974) The Shark Attack File

50' (15 m)	100' (30 m)	200' (60 m)	300' (90 m)	400' (120 m)	500' (150 m)	1000' (300 m)	1mile (1.6 km)	> 1 mile (> 1.6 km)

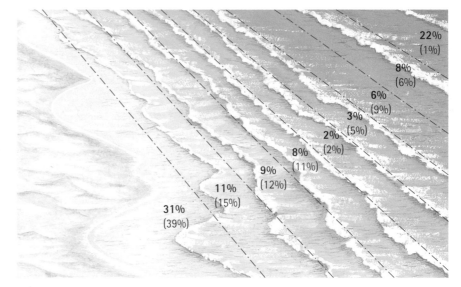

22% (1%)
8% (6%)
6% (9%)
3% (5%)
2% (2%)
8% (11%)
9% (12%)
11% (15%)
31% (39%)

LEFT: Statistics show that most shark attacks occur close to shore, which is not surprising given that most water users swim among the breakers. A more curious shark attack statistic is that men are 10 times more likely to be attacked than women. This presumably reflects historical trends in water use, although some researchers believe that behavioral differences, whether innate or cultural, may also play a role.

find their prey at the surface. Underwater attacks by sharks are not common. Nevertheless, given the relatively low number of people who venture underwater, the figures suggest that these people run a disproportionate risk of being attacked. Traditionally, spearfishers have been considered at particular risk of attack due to the amount of time they spend in the water, and the fact that sharks may be attracted by the blood and frenzied movements of injured fishes caught on their spearguns.

THE SITUATION TODAY

A breakdown of recent figures for shark attacks worldwide shows that swimmers are the most frequently attacked group, followed by surfers and boogie-boarders, spearfishers, snorkelers, scuba divers, anglers, and boaters. In Hawaii and Brazil, surfers and boogie-boarders have surpassed swimmers in recent years as the most attacked group of water users. These figures are not surprising given recent trends in recreational water use. The popularity of surfing and surf-related activities has increased dramatically since the 1950s, with people entering the ocean in ever-growing numbers.

Attacks on scuba divers, while still rare, have also increased in the last 15 years, and this can probably be attributed to the rapidly growing number of recreational divers using the ocean. Another possibility is the increased number of commercial divers involved in abalone or sea urchin fisheries that are located near white shark populations. At the same time, shark attacks on spearfishers appear to be declining. This may reflect a decline in the sport as a whole or may be the result of spearfishers being more careful about storing their bloody catch.

In some areas, shark attacks have increased despite a decline in shark numbers caused by overfishing and shark eradication programs. This does not suggest that sharks are becoming more aggressive, but rather it reflects the increasing number of people using the oceans for sport and recreation. Ironically, shark eradication programs (see page 135) may be partly responsible for a statistical rise in the number of attacks, with more people entering the water because they no longer feel at risk of attack.

ABOVE: Attacks on scuba divers are rare, although careless divers may find themselves the victim of provoked attacks if they deliberately or accidentally disturb a shark. Most sharks, however, are shy creatures, and will go out of their way to avoid contact with humans.

People stranded in the open ocean following boat or air disasters are particularly vulnerable to attack because they are often injured and bleeding, and they are floating at the surface with little protection.

Statistics show that more than 90 percent of reported shark attacks occur on the surface. This again reflects the habits of water users, but also suggests that feeding behavior may be an important factor in many attacks, as sharks often

DANGEROUS SHARKS

The following species are considered to be potentially dangerous.

White shark

Tiger shark

Bull shark

Oceanic whitetip shark

Blue shark

Bronze whaler

Shortfin mako

Great hammerhead

Dusky shark

Gray reef shark

Whitetip reef shark

Caribbean reef shark

Silky shark

Silvertip shark

Galapagos shark

SHARKS THAT ATTACK HUMANS

Sharks tend to attack as individuals rather than in groups, and it is not always possible to determine exactly what species was responsible for a given attack. However, while more than 30 species of shark have been implicated in attacks on humans, the vast majority of fatal attacks appear to be carried out by only three of these—the white, tiger, and bull sharks. What make these sharks dangerous to humans are their large size, their varied diet, their ability to capture large prey, and their tendency to inhabit those nearshore areas where people most often work and play.

White sharks are common along rocky shorelines where seals and sea lions crawl up onto the shore; areas also favored by surfers and divers. Tiger sharks are often found around shallow reefs, harbors, and stream mouths, and it is around such areas that people live in the greatest concentrations. Bull sharks, which are

normally considered a coastal species, are also found in locations where most people would not expect to find a shark, such as fresh-water rivers and estuaries. It should be noted, however, that none of these species includes humans as an important part of their diet and that aggressive encounters with any of them are rare.

The majority of open-ocean attacks are thought to be the work of oceanic whitetip sharks, although blue sharks are also thought to pose a risk to people stranded at sea. Non-fatal attacks near the shore have been attributed to smaller species, such as Caribbean and gray reef sharks. In many cases a surfer or swimmer has been bitten on the arm or foot—attacks termed "hit and runs" because the shark takes a bite, then flees. Such attacks may merely be cases of an inquisitive shark investigating a person in the water and then swimming off when it realizes that the victim was not the prey it was expecting.

ABOVE: The tiger shark is one of three species considered to pose a risk to humans, and is probably responsible for the majority of attacks in tropical waters. However, even a species such as this will not automatically attack a human when confronted. Dangerous is a relative term, and sharks are not particularly aggressive animals when compared to large terrestrial vertebrates. Realistically, water is a lot more dangerous for people than the sharks that inhabit it.

THE CHANCES OF ATTACK

Of the almost 500 species of shark, only 30 or so have been responsible for attacks on humans. So even if you swim in waters inhabited by sharks every day, the chances of being attacked are extremely low. Many more people are killed annually by dogs, crocodiles, bees, elephants, and even pigs than by sharks. Even in Australian waters, where the highest number of shark attacks per capita have been recorded, you are one hundred times more likely to drown than be attacked by a shark.

Of all recorded cases of shark attack, only about 30 percent have been fatal and fewer than 17 percent resulted in the removal of flesh. Furthermore, as the cause of death in most attacks is shock and loss of blood, fatalities have decreased tremendously in the last 50 years due to better and more rapid application of first aid, and the improved treatment of post-traumatic infection. The fatality rate for shark attacks

BELOW: The white shark is legendary for its attacks on humans and is believed to be the species most likely to attack people in temperate waters. However, it is often impossible to identify the species involved in an attack, and some researchers believe that white sharks are being unfairly blamed for attacks carried out by other species, such as the bull shark.

AVOIDING SHARK ATTACK

While the chances of being attacked by a shark are very low, there are a number of common-sense precautions you should take when swimming in areas inhabited by sharks.

• When visiting a new area, seek local advice.

• Always heed current shark warnings.

• Avoid swimming with an open wound; sharks may be attracted to blood and bodily fluids.

• Avoid swimming at dawn, dusk, and at night when sharks are most active.

• Avoid swimming alone.

• Don't wear jewelry when swimming; sharks may mistake it for the glinting scales of fish.

• Avoid areas where people are fishing.

• Avoid swimming in murky waters, particularly near flooding rivers.

• When spearfishing, store any catch carefully to avoid filling the water with blood.

• Never provoke a shark by attempting to touch it in any way.

• Learn to recognize when a shark is feeling threatened by your presence (see page 75).

reported during the last few years stands at around 20 percent. Nevertheless, it always pays to be cautious and there are a number of ways that you can reduce your chances of being attacked (see box).

If sharks attacks are so rare, why is there such an enduring fear of sharks? Perhaps it is because people don't understand them and cannot control them. On land we have established our dominance over every living creature, but in the water we are literally out of our depth and even our superior intellect cannot help us overcome what evolution has perfected over 450 million years. Whatever the reason, it is important to remind ourselves that sharks are only doing what they have always done in an environment where we are very much the intruders. While fatal shark attacks are tragic, the bottom line is that sharks have a lot more to fear from us than we do from them.

PROTECTING AGAINST SHARKS

Shark attacks have prompted a number of responses, ranging from fencing off beaches to attempting to eradicate the "problem." Some approaches focus on keeping sharks away from popular beaches, while others are aimed at protecting people once they are in the water.

SHARK-PROOFING BEACHES

In the past, attempts to keep swimmers and sharks apart have included the use of barriers such as metal and wood fences, electrical cables, and even a wall of bubbles emitted by a hose on the seabed. Expensive and difficult to maintain, none of these was widely used.

Following a recent spate of fatal attacks in Hong Kong, fine-mesh nets were installed along an entire beach. These nets effectively protected swimmers who stayed within them, and did not kill the sharks. Similar enclosures have been used successfully in Australia.

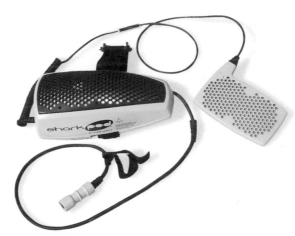

LEFT: The shark POD was designed to deter the three most dangerous sharks—the bull, great white, and tiger shark—and represents the most effective shark deterrent yet developed for divers. It takes advantage of a shark's sensitivity to electrical stimuli, generating a strong electric field around the diver.

A different approach has been to reduce the number of sharks in an area through eradication programs (see page 135). In South Africa, Australia, and Hawaii, nets and lines have been used to entangle and kill sharks off popular beaches. While such programs have reduced

BELOW: Beach nets, such as this one in Sydney Harbour, Australia, have been widely used to protect bathers. They are most effective when used at sheltered harbor beaches.

ABOVE: This diver is taking no chances with an inquisitive and potentially dangerous blue shark. Wearing a chain-mail suit and armed with a bang stick, the diver is well protected. While defensive devices such as the bang stick are effective, the harm they do to sharks detracts from their appeal to many divers.

Recently there has been an emphasis on deterrents that don't harm sharks. Designed to take advantage of sharks' keen senses, they have had little success. Killer whale sounds were tested to see if they could repel sharks, but while some species were deterred, others were unaffected. Colored wet suits resembling poisonous sea snakes were briefly investigated, but these were abandoned when it was realized that sea snakes are part of the tiger sharks' diet.

A great deal of research has gone into chemical repellents. The United States Navy experimented with a copper acetate repellent, and natural fish toxins and synthetic detergents have also been used, all without success. The limit to chemical repellents is that they disperse rapidly in water and are effective only when delivered directly into a shark's mouth.

One promising device recently developed by the Natal Sharks Board of South Africa is the POD (Protective Oceanic Device). This battery-powered device attaches to a scuba tank and produces an electric field around a person. When a shark encounters the field it is repelled and swims away, presumably unharmed. While initial results indicate that the POD is effective to a distance of about 23 feet (7 m), it remains to be seen whether it will be able to deter a large, highly motivated shark in feeding mode.

attacks, they are expensive and hugely destructive, killing not only sharks but also fishes, turtles, birds, and even whales.

UNDERWATER PROTECTIVE DEVICES

People have employed various methods to defend themselves from sharks, including shouting at them, punching them on the nose, and poking their eyes or gills. Although these people survived, it's impossible to know how many people tried such defenses unsuccessfully.

A more reliable approach to underwater protection is the use of stainless-steel dive suits and cages. Cages are popular with shark observers and professional abalone divers, but they are of little use to other water users. Of more use to recreational divers are anti-shark weapons, such as the "shark billy" and "bang stick." The shark billy is a pole with a sharp point to keep sharks at bay, while the bang stick is a pole with an explosive device that will kill a shark when banged against it. Lethal darts have also been developed, but these are rarely used. While the shark billy and bang stick continue to be used effectively, they have several drawbacks. They may injure the diver, they are of use only when a shark is seen as it approaches, and they may injure or kill the shark.

ABOVE: Shark cages are popular protective devices among professionals, and are also used by dive operators for close encounters with blue sharks off the coast of California. The drawback of cages is that they limit a diver's maneuverability.

WORKING WITH SHARKS

LEFT: During the last few decades, the emphasis of shark research has shifted from examining dead specimens to long-term experiments with live sharks in the wild. Here, a tiger shark is being tagged by researchers in the Bahamas so that information about its growth rate and movements can be gathered if it is recaptured in the future.

Until the last few decades, most of what we learned about sharks was derived from the study of dead specimens. By dissecting dead sharks, scientists were able to determine their internal anatomy, the structure of their skeletons and sensory systems, their diet, their method of tooth replacement, and their various reproductive strategies.

Some of the earliest studies of live sharks were funded by the United States Navy, which was concerned by the threats sharks posed to its personnel and equipment. This research focused on the sensory biology of sharks, with the ultimate goal being the development of an effective shark repellent. Much of this research was conducted in tanks or shallow pens near the shore, where the ability of sharks to see, smell, taste, and detect electric fields was tested. Open-ocean research included experiments to determine what sounds attract sharks and what provokes a threat display and consequent attack.

A SHIFT IN EMPHASIS

Whereas the research of the 1960s and 1970s was driven by the desire to protect humans from sharks, much of the research over the last 20 years has been inspired by the need to protect sharks from humans. As shark populations have declined, it has become increasingly important to learn more about their biology and patterns of migration so that the remaining populations can be protected and fishing can proceed on a sustainable basis.

Because sharks are large and their skin is thick and quick to heal, it is easy to fit them with transmitters and tags so they can be tracked and monitored over time. Consequently sharks have been at the forefront of both tagging and tracking technology, and procedures used on them have since been applied to other open-ocean fishes, including tuna and marlin.

LEFT: Research into live sharks is often conducted in shallow coastal waters. Here, a researcher is examining the flow of water through the olfactory system of a nurse shark. For the purposes of the experiment, the shark has been strapped to a frame.

TAGGING EXPERIMENTS

Tagging sharks can tell us how far they travel by comparing where a shark is tagged and where it is recaptured. This is important because it indicates how much of the ocean a particular species uses, and which country's fisheries are exploiting the same resource. Growth rates and longevity can also be determined by measuring a shark when it is tagged and when it is recaptured. Such information is vital for gauging the resilience of a species to fishing pressure and for calculating sustainable catch rates.

One particularly successful case of tagging is that of a soupfin shark tagged in 1949 off the south coast of Victoria, Australia and recaptured off Tasmania in 1991, 120 miles (194 km) away. Estimated to be 55 years old at the time of recapture, it had grown only 6¾ inches (17 cm) in the interceding period. Such figures confirm that sharks are slow-growing animals, and indicate just how vulnerable shark populations are to overfishing since they take so long to reach sexual maturity.

By far the most extensive shark tagging program was started by Jack Casey in 1961 off the New England coastline of the United States. In this ongoing program, more than 120,000 sharks of various species have been tagged and released by scientists, commercial fishermen, and anglers. The results have shown some remarkable long-distance migrations. One blue shark was recaptured 3,383 miles (5,450 km) away in the south Atlantic, a mako crossed from North America to Africa, and several tiger sharks made the 2,000 mile (3,220 km) trip from New England to the Gulf of Mexico.

TRACKING EXPERIMENTS

The limitation of tag-and-release experiments is that they tell us nothing about the shark's movements between the time it is tagged and when it is recaptured. To obtain more detailed information, transmitters have been placed on, or in, some sharks. Depth-sensitive transmitters allow us to measure not only the horizontal movements of sharks but also the depth and temperature at which they are located. Such data are important for understanding which parts of the ocean habitat the sharks use, and may ultimately help reduce shark bycatch and protect their nursery grounds.

BELOW: This diver is about to harpoon a tag into the skin of a blue shark. Shark skin is thick and fast healing, and tags are easily attached to it. In most cases, the shark does not even notice the tag being inserted.

Because radio waves do not penetrate salt water, transmitters for tracking sharks rely on ultrasound. Such transmitters only have a range of about 2,600 feet (800 m), which means that the tracking boat must stay close to the shark, not always an easy task in rough water.

Shark tracking was championed by Dr. Frank Carey who got off to an impressive start in 1979 when he found a group of white sharks feeding on a dead whale and was able to harpoon a transmitter into the back of a 15 foot (4.6 m) male. Over the next three and a half days he tracked the shark for 118 miles (190 km) off the coast of New York, observing that it oriented itself to temperature gradients in the water column and made frequent dives to the ocean floor.

Since then, many other species of shark have been tracked—from small hammerhead pups in their shallow nursery grounds to huge whale sharks basking at the surface. In each

case, the method used to attach the transmitter was adapted to suit the type of shark and the conditions in which it was found. Juvenile hammerheads can be caught and force-fed a transmitter through a tube, but in the cases of adult hammerheads and whale sharks, divers must harpoon the transmitters into place with spearguns, an apparently painless procedure.

An unusual approach is often used to attach transmitters to tiger sharks. For unknown reasons, sharks "go to sleep" when placed upside down (technically known as tonic immobility). Scientists can take advantage of this phenomenon to surgically implant large, long-life transmitters into a shark's abdominal

INSET: This juvenile lemon shark has been implanted with a sonic transmitter, which is monitored by a receiver on the seabed. BELOW: A shark tag is clearly visible attached to the back of this Caribbean reef shark. While such tags can remain in place for decades, there is always the danger that they will be dislodged during fights or even mating rituals.

feed, allowing them to be photographed from a boat. These photographs enable the sharks to be reliably identified years later, providing useful information about their distribution and migration patterns. An advantage of this method of identification over tagging is that the sharks need not be captured, and the problem of tags being shed is avoided.

While filming sharks has useful research applications, much of the work done in this area is aimed at the entertainment market. The growing popularity of television programs about sharks has encouraged some producers and cameramen to specialize in the area, going to great lengths and expense to obtain dramatic footage. Recent innovations in this area have included mounting downward-looking cameras inside surfboards to record the upward feeding charge of white sharks, and tethering miniature video cameras onto the backs of large sharks to provide a unique perspective of their world.

ABOVE: In their efforts to get the perfect shot, some divers take calculated risks. While this whale shark is not dangerous, a swipe from its enormous tail could result in injury.

ABOVE: To bring out the best in their subjects under low-light conditions, underwater photographers often use strobe lights attached to their camera housings. In this shot, artificial lighting has been used to highlight the features of a whitetip reef shark against the glare of the sun overhead. In the background another photographer can be seen with strobe lights attached to his camera.

cavity. In Hawaii, tracking of tiger sharks has shown that they cover large distances daily, they navigate expertly in the open ocean, and they can dive from the surface to 1,150 feet (350 m) and back again in just a few minutes.

FILMING AND PHOTOGRAPHING SHARKS

Film, video, and still photography are all used extensively in the study of sharks. By analysing high-speed video footage of sharks feeding, scientists have studied how sharks hunt and kill their prey. This approach was used to reveal the awesome biting action of the white shark, whereby it unhinges its jaws and thrusts them forward in a series of split-second movements.

Still photography has been used to identify individual white sharks, in an adaptation of a technique used for whales. The dorsal and caudal fins of white sharks have distinctive features that remain unchanged over time, and these fins break the water when the sharks

DIVING WITH SHARKS

The growing fascination with sharks is reflected in the increasing number of people paying to dive with them in their natural environment. Such dives usually involve sharks being attracted to a dive site with bait, or they take place in an area where sharks are known to gather in large numbers. Depending on the location, divers may see several different species and anywhere from one to more than 100 individual sharks.

ATTRACTING SHARKS WITH BAIT

Shark dives often involve sharks being offered a ball of bait suspended on a line, or sharks being hand fed by divers. Sometimes, if large sharks are present, cages may be used. Generally, however, sharks and divers mingle freely. Divers often begin such dives with their backs against an underwater wall, moving away from the wall once the feeding begins.

There are safety issues involved with such dives. Feeding sharks can be highly excited and there is a concern that sharks may learn to associate divers with food. However, these operations tend to have excellent safety records and a common impression that divers take away from such encounters is that the sharks were interested only in the bait, not the divers.

LEFT: A dive operator, well protected in a chain-mail suit, provokes a controlled feeding frenzy during a shark dive in the Bahamas. Although some people have questioned the wisdom of feeding sharks while other divers are nearby, these situations tend to be carefully controlled and perfectly safe. Nevertheless, you should always check the credentials of any diving operation before you commit yourself to a dive.

EXPLOITING NATURAL AGGREGATIONS

Other diving operations take advantage of natural aggregations of sharks. In places such as Cocos Island, off the west coast of Central America, scalloped hammerhead sharks school by the hundreds. In Rangiroa, Tahiti, large schools of reef sharks swim in a channel that

BELOW: This Caribbean reef shark is providing members of an organized shark dive with a memorable close encounter. Such dives are playing a vital role in changing people's perceptions of sharks.

POPULAR LOCATIONS FOR SHARK DIVES

Shark Junction, Grand Bahamas	Caribbean reef sharks
Shark Reef, Bahamas	Caribbean reef, nurse, bull, lemon sharks
Shark Hole, Bahamas	Caribbean reef, sharpnose, nurse sharks
Spiral Cave, Bahamas	Caribbean reef, bull, blacktip reef, lemon, nurse, silky sharks
Dirty Rock, Cocos Island	Scalloped and great hammerhead sharks
Manuelita Rock, Cocos Island	Whitetip reef, scalloped hammerhead, silky, Galapagos, oceanic whitetip sharks
El Bajo, Baja	Scalloped hammerhead, whale sharks
Gorda Banks, Baja	Scalloped hammerhead, silvertip, blacktip, tiger, whale sharks
California Bight, United States	Blue, mako sharks
Blue Corner, Palau	Gray reef, oceanic whitetip sharks
Tiputa Pass, Rangiroa, Tahiti	Gray reef, whitetip reef, lemon, hammerhead sharks
North Coral Sea, Papua New Guinea	Gray reef, great hammerhead sharks
Milne Bay, Papua New Guinea	Great and scalloped hammerhead sharks
Shark Pinnacle, Papua New Guinea	Silvertip sharks
Layang Layang Reef, Malaysia	Great hammerhead sharks
Silvertip Bank, Thailand	Nurse, whitetip reef, whale sharks
Daedalus Reef, Egypt	Hammerhead sharks
Rocky Island, Egypt	Scalloped, great hammerhead sharks
Flinders Reef, Australia	Whitetip reef, silvertip, hammerhead sharks
Osprey Reef, Australia	Whitetip reef, silvertip, tiger sharks
Great Detached Reef, Australia	Whitetip reef, silvertip, hammerhead, tiger sharks
Ningaloo Reef, Australia	Whale sharks
North Neptune Island, Australia	Great white sharks

a few hundred dollars to a fishery, people may pay a hundred dollars each time they dive with a live shark. With regular dives, and several people on each dive, shark dives have the potential to generate far greater revenue than the fishing industry, while having no impact whatsoever on shark numbers.

CHANGING PERCEPTIONS

Shark dives are serving a much greater purpose than just thrilling observers and generating income for dive operators—they are helping to profoundly alter people's perceptions of sharks. In the past, impressions of sharks were formed by lurid accounts of shark attacks, sensationalistic films such as *Jaws*, and images of dead sharks hanging by their tails, their sleek shapes distorted by gravity. The combined effect of such images was to provoke feelings of fear and revulsion in many observers. However, after viewing sharks in their natural environment, people tend to no longer see them as blood-thirsty killers, but rather as graceful, awe-inspiring animals.

With time, encounters with sharks may be seen in similar terms to encounters with bears, tigers, and wolves—animals that were once feared and hunted but which are now considered beautiful, valuable, and in need of protection from human interference. Such a change in people's perceptions of sharks, combined with an understanding of the role of sharks in the marine ecosystem, may be the most important factors driving shark conservation in the 1990s and beyond.

RIGHT: When viewing large or potentially dangerous sharks, cages are often used to ensure the safety of participants. Here, blue sharks are being observed by Japanese tourists in waters off San Diego in the United States.

connects a lagoon to the open ocean, and pay little attention to divers who come to watch them. Divers in such locations get to watch sharks swimming calmly and peacefully in their natural environment, and take away from the experience a greater understanding of the role of sharks in their underwater world.

BETTER ALIVE THAN DEAD

One of the most positive aspects of shark dives in terms of shark conservation, is that such operations make very good economic sense. While a dead shark may be worth only

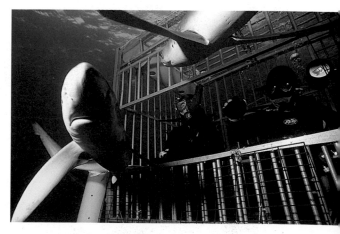

SHARKS IN CAPTIVITY

Sharks have been kept in captivity since the late 1800s and techniques for keeping them have improved greatly over the years. Not long ago, sharks were considered expendable. It was easier to replace a shark than to keep it alive for a long time, so they were caught, displayed, and then replaced when they died, with little regard for their well being.

THE SITUATION TODAY

These days, great care is taken to monitor the health of sharks in captivity and to make sure they have an appropriate diet. At some aquariums sharks receive regular check-ups, including blood sampling and treatment for parasites and diseases. The construction and design of shark tanks have also come a long way in the last 15 years. Special consideration is now given to the way in which sharks swim, with tanks being constructed in the shape of a figure-eight rather than a rectangle.

Sharks are expensive to catch, and with some major aquariums hundreds of miles from the ocean, they are also expensive to transport.

Specially designed tanks are used to transport captured sharks by boat, truck, and even plane. As a result, every shark kept in captivity represents a considerable financial investment. Fortunately, this provides an incentive for aquariums to treat their sharks well and avoid having to replace them prematurely.

In the United States alone, there are more than 40 species of shark on display at aquariums, ranging in size from one foot (30 cm) long bamboo sharks to 60 feet (18.3 m) long whale sharks. Some species, such as lemon, blacktip reef, whitetip reef, sand tiger, bull, zebra, and leopard sharks, have adapted well to life in captivity and survived for many years. Some have even mated and reproduced in tanks.

Not all sharks, however, are suited to a life in captivity. White sharks have only ever been kept for a few days before they died or were released. A few tiger sharks have survived for several years in aquariums, but most have died after a short time or have been released. The major limitation to keeping these species is tank size—aquarium tanks simply aren't large enough to accommodate large, free-ranging sharks that require a large body of water in which to swim.

THE CASE FOR CAPTIVITY

Sharks in the wild are difficult to observe for a number of reasons. They range widely, they may be dangerous, and they live in a concealing medium. Therefore, it is not surprising that much of our knowledge of sharks is based on studies or observations of captive sharks, both at research laboratories and public aquariums. Recently these studies have contributed a great deal to our knowledge of the reproduction, diseases, and physiology of sharks.

Just as importantly, displaying live sharks in aquariums gives people the opportunity to appreciate their beauty and grace in a simulation of their natural environment. While many people do not have the time, money, or inclination to dive with sharks in the open sea (see pages 148–149), most people have access to aquariums. Making sharks accessible to the community at large may be the key to changing perceptions of sharks and generating widespread public support for their conservation.

LEFT: Capturing a live shark for an aquarium is a delicate and costly operation. To ensure that sharks are not injured they are often lassoed at sea and constrained in a sling. Once secured, they are sedated and placed in a small, self-contained tank so they can be safely transported to the aquarium.

RIGHT: *While this captive sand tiger shark is gentle enough to be hand fed, sharks are highly instinctive and can never be considered tame. Although captive sharks are rarely released, there is little doubt they would survive in the wild if they were.*

BELOW: *This tiger shark from the Bahamas is one of few kept in captivity. Such large, free-ranging sharks tend not to adapt well to a constrained, captive environment.*

THE CASE AGAINST CAPTIVITY

Those who object to sharks being kept in captivity claim that it is cruel to keep them in an unnatural environment and that confinement can affect their behavior, reproduction, and, most importantly, their chances of survival. It has also been noted that there are limits to what extent we can extrapolate from studies of captive sharks to those in the wild. Reproductive studies, in particular, do not accurately reflect the situation for wild sharks. As a result, data from captive sharks have limited application to fishery management plans.

Despite these limitations, however, our understanding of sharks has increased enormously as a result of studying captive sharks. And while the captive environment is undoubtedly a restrictive one, it is perhaps a tradeoff between doing a disservice to a specific animal and benefiting sharks as a whole. The more people know about sharks the less their judgment of them will be clouded by misinformation and prejudice. Ultimately, this can only benefit all sharks.

CONSERVATION AND SURVIVAL

LEFT: This gray reef shark has been caught in a net in waters off Thailand. As sharks take several years to reach sexual maturity, have a long gestation period, and don't reproduce in high numbers, it could take decades or even longer for there to be sufficient numbers of certain species to ensure their continued survival.

Shark populations are declining worldwide at alarming rates due to overfishing. In some cases sharks are the intended target of fishing operations but in many other cases they represent unintended bycatch (see pages 132–135). During the 1970s, at the height of a media-driven demonization of sharks, government agencies were promoting sharks as an underutilized resource. As a result sharks were harvested with increasing frequency in a climate of ignorance and misinformation. Today many shark populations are so depleted that fishermen can no longer make a living from them. As more and more shark populations decline, the conservation of sharks is becoming a serious global issue.

A LACK OF INFORMATION

Efforts to develop adequate management strategies for shark fishing are hampered by a lack of critical information about the basic biology, ecology, and behavior of many species. Such information includes longevity, breeding patterns, migratory routes, and location of nursery grounds. Although our understanding of sharks has increased enormously in recent times, the picture remains far from complete.

Several countries that have heavily exploited their shark stocks have attempted to rectify the problem by introducing quotas and restrictions on the numbers of sharks that can be caught within their waters. However, as many species of shark are migratory and do not recognize arbitrary national boundaries, they remain susceptible to overfishing when they leave waters where such restrictions apply.

WHAT CAN BE DONE?

As sharks are being killed for so many reasons, there is no single solution to the decline in their numbers. One solution to the problem of limited quotas and restrictions would be to develop and enforce a global approach to shark management, perhaps in the same way the United Nations successfully banned the use of driftnets on the high seas. Other important conservation measures may include developing techniques and fishing gear that reduce the numbers of sharks caught incidentally by fisheries targeting other fishes. Unfortunately, any attempt to radically overhaul fishing methods would be likely to encounter stiff resistance from commercial operators.

CONSUMER EDUCATION

The most effective approach to shark conservation may come through consumer education and marketing. Although most people know that sharks are fishes, many still do not know that sharks' longevity and rates of reproduction differ from those of other fishes and that consequently sharks cannot be harvested in the same quantities. Since consumers are the ones who generate the demand for a product, an educated consumer might decide that their need for shark products is not great enough to cause the demise of shark populations. Even the bycatch problem could be addressed by consumer boycotts, such as those targeted at driftnet fishing operations in response to the accidental killing of dolphins.

We are presently witnessing a shift in the way people view sharks, from a sinister and expendable resource to a fascinating and ecologically vital inhabitant of our oceans. Even the world's most maligned shark, the great white, is now legally protected from fishing in the United States, South Africa, and Australia because of its ecological importance and declining numbers. However, much work remains to be done. It would be tragic if we were responsible for the demise of creatures that have survived so many calamitous upheavals over the past 450 million years.

BELOW: This blue shark is lucky to be alive after an encounter with a gillnet. Swimming freely with the remnants of the net around its neck, it represents a rare victory for sharks in their ongoing struggle against human interference.
INSET: The demand for shark products, such as these tails, continues to grow, taking a relentless toll on shark stocks.

GLOSSARY

ADELOPHAGY A form of uterine cannibalism whereby one of more embryos survive by eating their siblings.

AGONISTIC Aggressive or combative; usually in reference to behavior.

BARBELS Slender fleshy protuberances, usually near the nostrils, that have a sensory function, the exact nature of which is unknown.

BENTHIC Bottom dwelling.

BIOLUMINESCENCE The production of light by living organisms; common in many deep-water sharks.

BRANCHIAL Relating to the gills.

BYCATCH Fishes caught incidentally by fishing operations that are targeting other species.

CAUDAL KEEL A fleshy ridge running along the base of a shark's tail.

CETACEANS Whales, dolphins and porpoises.

CEPHALOPODS A class of mollusks, including squid and octopus.

CHEMOSENSORY Having a sensory sensitivity to chemicals.

CHROMATOPHORE Pigment cells in a shark's skin that produce skin colors and patterns.

CHUM Collective term for the various baits used to attract and feed sharks.

CLASPERS The external reproductive organs of male sharks.

The claspers of this male sand tiger shark are clearly visible on its underside

CLOACA Combined reproductive and excretory cavity.

CRUSTACEANS Creatures with chitinous exoskeletons, including barnacles, krill, copepods, crabs, shrimps, and prawns.

DENTICLES The tooth-like scales attached to a shark's skin.

DENTITION The type and arrangement of teeth.

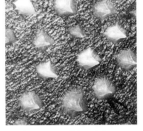

Close-up of denticles on the skin of a Greenland sleeper shark

DERMIS The inner layer of a shark's skin, comprised of cells in a network of tissue fibers.

ECHINODERMS A group of radially symmetrical creatures, including sea stars, sea cucumbers, and sea urchins.

ECOLOGY The science focusing on the relationship between organisms and their environment.

ECTOTHERMIC Having a variable internal temperature that is warmed or cooled externally; also known as exothermic.

ELASMOBRANCH The group of cartilaginous fishes comprising the sharks and rays.

ENDOTHERMIC Internally warmed.

EPIDERMIS The outer layer of a shark's skin, composed of multiple layers of cells.

EPIPELAGIC Inhabiting the upper levels of the ocean.

FINNING The practice of cutting the fins off sharks, often while they are still alive.

GILL FILAMENTS Thin, plate-like structures, rich with blood vessels, that allow the exchange of oxygenated water and waste during respiration.

GILLNETS Underwater fishing nets used to ensnare sharks and other fishes by their head and gills, or body and fins.

GILL RAKERS Specialized, tooth-like structures inside the gill slits for straining particles from the water.

GILL SEPTA The vertical, plate-like partition between the gills, supported by a cartilaginous gill arch and gill rays.

GILL SLITS The external openings of the gill system.

HOLOCEPHALAN The group of cartilaginous fishes comprising chimaeras.

INSULAR Pertaining to islands.

INTERTIDAL The area that falls between the limits of low and high tide.

INVERTEBRATES All animals without backbones.

LABIAL FURROWS Grooves around the lips of some sharks.

LATERAL LINE A system of paired sensory tubes, running beneath a shark's skin from the head to the base of the caudal fin, that is involved in the detection of vibrations in the water.

LITTORAL Pertaining to the coast; adapted to an active, coastal existence.

LONGLINES Underwater fishing lines with multiple branches, each baited with a hook.

MACROPREDATORY Large animals that actively hunt other animals.

MESHING Setting large, wide-meshed gillnets parallel to beaches to catch sharks.

MICRO-NICHE A small habitat within a larger ecological system.

NEUROMASTS Sensory cells with hair-like protrusions, which are sensitive to vibrations in the water.

NICTITATING MEMBRANE A tough inner eyelid that protects the eyes of certain sharks when feeding.

OCELLUS An eye-like spot or marking.

OOPHAGY A form of uterine cannibalism whereby developing embryos feed on unfertilized eggs.

OVIPARITY A form of reproduction whereby eggs are laid in cases and the embryo is sustained by the yolk.

A recently hatched swellshark, an oviparous species of shark

OVOVIVIPARITY The most common form of reproduction whereby the egg is encased but remains inside the shark's body; also known as retained oviparity or aplacental viviparity.

PAPILLAE Small, fleshy projections, such as those on the tongue.

PELAGIC Swimming freely in the open ocean; not associated with the bottom.

PERICARDIAL CAVITY The body cavity that contains the heart.

PHARYNX The mouth cavity.

PHOTOPHORES Luminous organs on deep-water fishes.

This close-up view of the eye of a catshark clearly reveals the nictitating membrane

PIT ORGANS Small, blind pockets in the skin, containing hair cells, which are sensitive to vibrations in the water. Pit organs, which are protected by pairs of denticles, are associated with, but not connected to, the lateral line.

PLACENTAL VIVIPARITY The form of reproduction whereby uncased embryos remain inside the mother until birth, during which time they are sustained by way of a placenta.

PLACOID Plate-like; used in reference to a shark's dermal denticles.

PLANKTON Minute animals or plants that drift in the open sea. Animal plankton is known as zooplankton; plant plankton is known as phytoplankton.

PLEUROPERITONAL CAVITY The trunk cavity containing internal organs.

POSTERIOR MARGIN The rear edge; in reference to fins.

PRECAUDAL PIT A notch just in front of the caudal fin.

SPIRACLE An auxiliary respiratory opening behind the eyes.

SUBTERMINAL NOTCH An indentation along the lower margin of the upper lobe of the caudal fin.

SUCTORIAL Adapted for sucking.

SYMBIOSIS Any close relationship between two organisms that is beneficial to at least one of them.

TOP PREDATOR An animal that is at the top of the food chain and is usually not preyed upon by any other animal.

TRICUSPID Having three cusps; in reference to teeth.

UPWELLING A column of water moving vertically toward the surface.

VERTEBRATES All animals that have a backbone, or spinal column.

VISCERAL CAVITY The trunk cavity containing internal organs; also known as the pleuroperitonal cavity.

VIVIPAROUS A form of reproduction whereby young develop inside the mother's body; sometimes used as a synonym for placental viviparity.

YOLK-SAC VIVIPARITY A form of reproduction whereby sharks are retained within the mother, encased within a very thin membrane.

Ceremonial shark carvings once used by natives of the Solomon Islands

INDEX

Bold page numbers indicate the main reference while figures in italics indicate photographs, illustrations, and captions.

CONTRIBUTORS AND PICTURE CREDITS

CONTRIBUTORS

LEONARD J.V. COMPAGNO Dr. Compagno is the Curator of Fishes and Head of the Shark Research Center at the South African Museum, where he specializes in the systematics, evolution, morphology, distribution, conservation, and general biology of sharks, rays, and chimaeras. He has written more than 100 scientific papers, popular articles, and books about cartilaginous fishes, including the 1984 *FAO Catalog of World Sharks*. He is a long-term consultant to the Food and Agriculture Organization of the United Nations and a regional vice-chair of the IUCN Shark Specialist group, an international panel of experts that advises on shark conservation.

KIM HOLLAND Dr. Holland is an Associate Researcher at the Hawaii Institute of Marine Biology where he is Director of the Shark Research Group. This group includes graduate students Chris Lowe, Brad Wetherbee, Aaron Bush, and Carl Meyer, who are conducting various shark experiments under Dr. Holland's guidance and who all contributed material to this book.

JOHN E. MCCOSKER Dr. McCosker is currently Senior Scientist and Chair of Aquatic Biology at the California Academy of Sciences, San Francisco, in the United States. Trained as an evolutionary biologist, his current research activities include the predatory behavior of the great white shark. Dr. McCosker has published numerous articles about sharks in books and scientific journals.

COLIN SIMPFENDORFER Dr. Simpfendorfer is currently leading a research team at the Fisheries Department of Western Australia, studying shark biology, fisheries, and population assessment. He is also a member of the IUCN's Shark Specialist Group and has contributed numerous articles about sharks to scientific journals and other publications.

CAPTIONS

Page 1 An oceanic whitetip shark viewed from below in Hawaiian waters.

Page 2 A gray reef shark swimming at Beveridge Reef in the South Pacific Ocean.

Page 3 A speckled carpetshark searching for prey near the sea floor.

Pages 6–7 Pregnant Port Jackson sharks in shallow water off the east coast of Australia.
Inset: A great white shark lunging out of the water.

Pages 22–3 A snaggletooth shark resting under a ledge at the Burma Banks in the Andaman Sea.
Inset: Spiny lobsters off the Californian coast.

Pages 38–9 The external gill slits of a whale shark, open to expel deoxygenated water.
Inset: The eye of a blacktip shark.

Pages 64–5 A variety of shark species in a feeding frenzy off Cape Cuvier, Western Australia.
Inset: A swellshark embryo in its egg case.

Pages 86–7 A scalloped hammerhead in waters near the Galapagos Islands.
Inset: The snout of a California hornshark

Pages 124–5 A group of divers observing a blacktip shark at Walker's Cay in the Bahamas.
Inset: A diver with an angelshark.